MANIFEST ACTIVITY

Thomas Reid's Theory of Action

THE UNIVERSITY OF
WINCHESTER

M
of
pl
ph
th
di
st
re

Fo
tha
ou
co
fro
the
He
dir
the
me
hu
hu
Pat
in
for

Ma
im
cau
me
fre

Gideon Yaffe is Associate Professor of Philosophy and Law at the University
of Southern California.

Manifest Activity

Thomas Reid's Theory of Action

Gideon Yaffe

CLARENDON PRESS · OXFORD

OXFORD
UNIVERSITY PRESS

Great Clarendon Street, Oxford OX2 6DP

Oxford University Press is a department of the University of Oxford.
It furthers the University's objective of excellence in research, scholarship,
and education by publishing worldwide in

Oxford New York

Auckland Bangkok Buenos Aires Cape Town Chennai
Dar es Salaam Delhi Hong Kong Istanbul Karachi Kolkata
Kuala Lumpur Madrid Melbourne Mexico City Mumbai Nairobi
São Paulo Shanghai Taipei Tokyo Toronto

Oxford is a registered trade mark of Oxford University Press
in the UK and in certain other countries

Published in the United States
by Oxford University Press Inc., New York

British Library Cataloguing in Publication Data

Data available

Library of Congress Cataloging in Publication Data

Data available

ISBN 978-0-19-926855-9 (Hbk.)   978-0-19-922803-4 (Pbk.)

1 3 5 7 9 10 8 6 4 2
Typeset by Laserwords Private Limited, Chennai, India
Printed in Great Britain
on acid-free paper by
Biddles Ltd., King's Lynn, Norfolk

For Sue

A man in love naturally and insensibly falls into the imitation
of the qualities he loves.

Thomas Reid, *Practical Ethics*, p. 224

Acknowledgements

Although I didn't know it at the time, this project began in 1998 while I was teaching at the University of California at San Diego. Since then, a very large number of people have helped me with it, some of whom probably don't even remember the help they gave. Terence Cuneo, James Harris, Paul Hoffman, Ryan Nichols, and James Van Cleve were all particularly generous with their time, reading, and sometimes rereading, large sections of the manuscript. I've also benefited from careful comments on parts of the manuscript, and on ancestors of parts of the manuscript, from all of the following people: Michael Bratman, Sarah Buss, Vere Chappell, Randy Clarke, John Fischer, Jennifer Rosner, and William Rowe. Thanks are also owed to the following people who provided encouragement, conversation, and sometimes well-timed quizzical looks: David Brink, Rebecca Copenhaver, David Cunning, John Dreher, Steve Finlay, Harry Frankfurt, Roger Gallie, Judy Genova, Brian Glenney, Peter Graham, Gordon Graham, Sean Greenberg, Mara Harrell, James Higginbotham, Walter Hopp, Robin Jeshion, Nick Jolley, Esther Kroeker, Jonathan Lee, Keith Lehrer, Janet Levin, Ed McCann, Bob McJimsey, P. D. Magnus, Adrienne Martin, Wayne Martin, Alan Nelson, Michael Nelson, David Owen, Michael Pakaluk, Andy Reath, John Riker, Victoria Rogers, Marleen Rozemond, Alison Simmons, Houston Smit, J. C. Smith, Dan Speak, Peter Thielke, Iain Thompson, Kadri Vihvelin, Gary Watson, Howie Wettstein, Dallas Willard, Nicholas Wolterstorff, Daniel Yim, Andrew Youpa, and Sherri Zhu. Thanks are also owed to Peter Momtchiloff and Alison Heard of Oxford University Press who were of tremendous help in smoothing the way for the book's publication.

Various pieces of the material that found their way into the book were presented in the following places, and thanks are owed to helpful audiences at each presentation: the Reid Symposium at the University of Aberdeen, the University of California at Irvine, the Southern California Philosophy Conference at California State University at Long Beach, James Van Cleve's summer NEH seminar on Reid, Colorado College, the University of California at Riverside, and the ISECS conference in 2003.

James Van Cleve's seminar on Reid in the summer of 2000 was a turning point in my thinking about Reid, and thanks are owed to all of its participants and to the National Endowment for the Humanities for funding the seminar. I'm also particularly thankful to the University of Southern California, where I work, and the American Council of Learned Societies. Funding from these institutions made it possible for me to have an invaluable year away from teaching during which the book was written and revised.

Contents

References to Reid's Works

COR   *The Correspondence of Thomas Reid*, ed. P. Wood (University Park, Pa.: Pennsylvania State University Press, 2002). References are by letter number and page number.

EAP   *Essays on the Active Powers of Man*, ed. B. Brody (Cambridge, Mass.: MIT Press, 1969). References to all essays other than essay III are by essay, chapter, and page number. References to essay III are by essay, section, chapter, and page number. The second page number given is to the corresponding page and column (*a* for left, *b* for right) in vol. ii of *The Works of Thomas Reid, D.D.*, ed. W. Hamilton, 6th edn., 2 vols. (Edinburgh: MacLachlan & Stewart, 1872).

EIP   *Essays on the Intellectual Powers of Man*, ed. D. Brookes (University Park, Pa.: Pennsylvania State University Press, 2002). References are by essay, chapter, and page number.

INQ   *An Inquiry into the Human Mind: On the Principles of Common Sense*, ed. D. Brookes (University Park, Pa.: Pennsylvania State University Press, 1997). References are by chapter, section, and page number.

OP   "Of Power", *The Philosophical Quarterly*, 51/202 (Jan. 2001), 3–12. References are by page number.

TAC   *Thomas Reid on the Animate Creation: Papers Relating to the Life Sciences*, ed. P. Wood (University Park, Pa.: Pennsylvania State University Press, 1995). References are by page number.

Introduction: Teleology and the Science of Action

Thomas Reid was a devoted "natural philosopher" in the sense in which that term was used in the seventeenth and eighteenth centuries. He was, that is, as dedicated to solving problems that we now consider to be in the domain of natural science as he was to solving traditional philosophical problems. Like most natural philosophers, he did not recognize a sharp division between the questions of natural science and those of philosophy. He subscribed to a model of correct scientific inquiry inherited from Bacon, Newton, Boyle, and Locke and expounded most influentially, in Britain, by the Royal Society. But he made every effort to follow this very method in his investigation of those problems that we now think of as lying in the domain of philosophy, and outside of the domain of the natural sciences. This book concerns Reid's effort to develop a science of human action; it concerns, that is, his efforts to provide answers to a host of traditional philosophical questions concerning the nature of the will, the powers of human beings, motivation, and the relation between human action and natural change, through employing what he took to be the correct methods of scientific inquiry.

Reid's *Essays on the Active Powers of Man* is the most important work in which he makes progress on his science of human action, although he strays into discussion of such issues in his *Inquiry into the Human Mind: On the Principles of Common Sense*, in his *Essays on the Intellectual Powers of Man*, in his correspondence, and in some essays not published during his lifetime. This book offers a critical examination of the claims and arguments Reid offers in these works, and understands them as efforts to make scientific contributions to our understanding of our capacities for action, and our place within the natural order, in the distinctively eighteenth-century sense in which he understood such contributions.

Reid's philosophy of action and model of human agency are developed in opposition to the "Necessitarian" tradition of thought about such issues. The Necessitarians hold that human actions are just like other events to be found in nature. If they exhibit any special properties—if we are, for instance, free when we act, or genuinely active authors of the behaviors in which we engage—then these properties are, despite appearances, entirely compatible with our actions being of the same sort as the behaviors of sticks and stones, plants and animals; in particular, the distinctive features of human actions are compatible with those actions being "necessitated", or causally determined. (Although, arguably, there were Necessitarians in the period who denied that human actions have these special properties at all, the varieties of Necessitarianism that are of greatest interest here are those closest to the contemporary view labeled "Compatibilism".) Necessitarianism was often advocated by those who, if not staunch materialists, at least allowed the possibility that the mind was an entirely material entity, and allowed the possibility that thoughts of all sorts were merely modifications of matter of the very same kind as shape, size, and motion. For the Necessitarians, freedom and the activity (as opposed to passivity) which our actions manifestly possess are properties no more mysterious or unaccountable than the ordinary physical properties possessed by the objects that surround us.

While Reid knew and opposed the Necessitarian views of Hobbes, Locke, Locke's follower Anthony Collins, and Hume, he was particularly enraged by the Necessitarianism advocated by his rival Joseph Priestley.[1] Although part of what angered Reid was Priestley's dismissive attitude towards him—he describes Reid at one point as a "pretended Philosopher"[2]— he was more concerned with Priestley's contention that Necessitarianism was the only view of human agency that could be accepted consistent with adherence to the scientific method expounded by Newton. Rather, Reid

---

[1] Cf. Thomas Hobbes, "Of Liberty and Necessity" and "The Questions Concerning Liberty, Necessity and Chance, Clearly Stated and Debated Between Dr. Bramhall, Bishop of Derry, and Thomas Hobbes of Malmesbury", in *The English Works of Thomas Hobbes*, iv (Aalen: Scientia, 1648); John Locke, *An Essay Concerning Human Understanding*, ed. P. H. Nidditch (Oxford: Clarendon Press, 1975), II. XXI, pp. 233–87; Anthony Collins, *A Philosophical Inquiry Concerning Human Liberty*, (Bristol: Thoemmes, 1990); David Hume, *Treatise of Human Nature*, ed. D. F. Norton and M. J. Norton (Oxford: Oxford University Press, 2000), II. iii. 1–2, pp. 257–65; Joseph Priestley, *The Doctrine of Philosophical Necessity Illustrated* (New York: Garland Press, 1976). For a very useful discussion of the relationship between Reid and Priestley, see Paul Wood's introduction to *TAC*, esp. pp. 30–56.

[2] Joseph Priestley, *An Examination of Dr. Reid's Inquiry into the Human Mind on the Principles of Common Sense, Dr. Beattie's Essay on the Nature and Immutability of Truth, and Dr. Oswald's Appeal to Common Sense in Behalf of Religion* (London, 1774), 5.

holds, the methods of Newton lead to a very different view of human agency than that advocated by the Necessitarians.

Reid considers the primary aim, but not the *only* aim, of scientific inquiry of the sort practiced by Newton to be the identification of the basic laws according to which particular phenomena come about. Often, the law under which a particular fact, or set of facts, is first subsumed is not a basic law but, instead, an instance of a more general law. For instance, we might subsume the fact that a particular equilateral triangle has angles adding up to 180 degrees under the law, "Planar equilateral triangles have angles adding up to 180 degrees." This law could then be deduced from a more general law, not limited to equilateral triangles, "Planar triangles have angles that add up to 180 degrees." This more general law is, in turn, deducible from a yet more general law: the equation stating the sum of the angles of a convex planar figure as a function of the number of sides of the figure ($180 * (n - 2)$). Even this law is not basic since it is provable through appeal to the axioms of Euclidean geometry; it can be deduced, that is, from those axioms.

Empirical inquiries have precisely the same structure. A set of observations are subsumed under a law, which is then deduced from a more general law, until a basic law, or set of laws, analogous to the axioms of geometry, is identified. The law "Unsupported objects fall towards the earth", for instance, is deduced ultimately from equations describing gravitational attraction, equations, that is, for the relative motion of objects as a function of the mass of each. And perhaps these equations, too, are deducible from yet more general laws. The basic laws, those from which others are deduced and which are not, themselves, deducible from any more general laws, are what Reid calls "first principles". So, the primary aim of scientific inquiry is the identification of first principles and the deduction of particular facts from those first principles.[3]

[3] In both the scientific explanation of necessary truths, such as the truths of mathematics, and in the scientific explanation of contingent truths, such as the truths about everyday observable events, the propositions to be explained are *deduced* from the first principles. The propositions to be explained are logically entailed by the first principles that the scientist identifies. The difference between necessary truths and contingent truths derives from a difference in the modal status of the first principles from which they are deducible: necessary truths are deducible from necessary first principles, contingent from contingent. Reid is clear that the term "first principles" can be used interchangeably with the term "principles of common sense" (cf. *EIP* VI. 4, p. 452). Given this, it might seem strange to claim that for him the basic laws of nature are first principles. After all, basic laws are not always dictated by common sense; they need to be discovered through observation and experiment. However, Reid's favorite examples of the first principles of contingent truths—such as the law of universal gravitation (cf. *EIP* VI. 4, p. 456)— are basic laws of nature.

Reid often describes first principles as principles to which we cannot but give our assent, assuming that we allow our assent to be guided by our natures as human beings, and not by acquired biases. He writes, for instance:

All reasoning must be from first principles; and for first principles no other reason can be given but this, that, by the constitution of our nature, we are under a necessity of assenting to them. Such principles are parts of our constitution, no less than the power of thinking: reason can neither make nor destroy them; nor can it do anything without them. (*INQ* 5. 7, p. 71)

What this implies is that first principles are not accepted on rational grounds, even if it is rational to accept them. We do not believe a particular first principle to be true because we recognize some more general fact, which we believe, and which implies it; this is what would be required if a first principle were to be accepted on the basis of reason. However, it is important to see that this does not imply that first principles cannot be demonstrated, a common misconception about Reid's view of first principles. Reid holds, rather, that first principles cannot be *proven*. A proof is an argument for a proposition that gives one greater epistemic reason to accept the proposition than one would have had in the absence of the argument; a demonstration is an argument for a proposition that offers premises from which the proposition is deduced. Sometimes the premises from which a proposition can be deduced are more certain than the proposition itself, and in these cases the demonstration serves as a proof of the proposition. But not all demonstrations are proofs, and, in fact, no demonstration of a first principle is a proof of it. Reid holds that, although we can demonstrate many first principles, the demonstrations that can be offered for them give us no greater reason to assent to those propositions than we had in the absence of the demonstration.

However, the fact that we do not accept first principles on the basis of reasons does not imply that scientific inquiry simply stops at the point that first principles are identified. For one thing, first principles can be denied, so anyone who claims to have identified a first principle needs to show that people who deny it explicitly are actually committed to it implicitly, either by something else they believe, or by their conduct. Second, a principle can be accepted and yet it can be denied that it is a *first* principle on the grounds that it is actually accepted on the basis of reasons. So, anyone who claims to have identified a first principle also needs to show that people accept it non-inferentially. Thus demonstrating that people naturally and non-inferentially accept a particular putative first principle is itself part of what the natural philosopher must do.

In addition, new truths can be discovered by deducing them from first principles discovered through some independent means. Just as the axioms of arithmetic or geometry can be used to prove previously unknown theorems, even though the axioms were discovered as the grounds from which known truths follow, so new truths in any domain can be discovered once a set of first principles is identified. So, the deduction of new truths from discovered first principles is also part of proper scientific methodology. Most explicitly in the *Essays on the Active Powers*, Reid tries to identify first principles concerning the powers of human beings, and the powers behind natural change; he argues that those principles are accepted even by those who purport to deny them; he argues that they are accepted non-inferentially; and he makes every effort to deduce previously unknown truths from the first principles he identifies. In so doing, he takes himself to be following the very methods of correct inquiry prescribed by Newton.

However, even a complete enumeration of the laws under which phenomena fall, and a complete accounting of the first principles governing them, is not all that the devoted Newtonian aims to provide, Reid thinks. The devoted Newtonian also describes the metaphysical structures that must underlie the fundamental principles according to which phenomena unfold. Thus, for Reid, to be a Newtonian is not to be a narrow empiricist; experience provides the basis for much of what one is licensed to assert about the world, but the Newtonian must also determine what must be true, what the structure of the world must be like, if experience is to be subsumed under law. For Reid, this further project is intertwined with his attitude towards Hume's view of causation. While widely known as a critic of Hume, Reid nonetheless accepts what he takes to be the moral of Hume's negative arguments about causation: "We see events, but we see not the power that produces them. We perceive one event to follow another, but we see not the chain that binds them together. The notion of power and causation, therefore, cannot be got from external objects" (*EAP* IV. 6, p. 305/617*a–b*). Reid agrees with Hume that we have no sensory impressions of power or the causal tie between events. However, as Reid understands him, Hume conjoins this point with the further view that all our ideas are "copied" from our sensory impressions and thereby derives a positive position that Reid rejects: to call something a cause is merely to claim that there is a law that says that things like it are always followed by things like the effect (cf. *EAP* IV. 2, p. 271/604*b*; IV. 3, p. 281/608*a*; IV. 9, pp. 333–5/627a–b; *COR* 93, pp. 173–4). Following Reid, call things that count as causes and effects in this sense "physical causes" and "physical effects".[4] To claim that one event is the physical cause of another is to claim no more nor less than that there is a law that says that the second will follow the first. Reid allows that we are often concerned to identify those events that count as the "cause", in this weak, Humean sense, of observed events. And he thinks that the notion of physical causation is central both to everyday life and to the natural sciences (cf. *INQ* 6. 12, p. 122; *EAP* I. 5, p. 33/522b; IV. 3, p. 279/607a; *TAC* 190). By knowing what will follow what, we maneuver our way towards our ends over the obstacles the world throws at us; and it is in efforts to identify the laws of nature that we are occupied in scientific endeavors.

As important as physical causation is, however, to identify only the physical causes would leave an important aspect of the world undescribed; a complete enumeration of all of the laws governing phenomena, that is, would not amount to a complete description of the world:

[S]upposing that all the phenomena that fall within the reach of our senses, were accounted for from the general laws of nature, justly deduced from experience; that is, supposing natural philosophy brought to its utmost perfection, it does not discover the efficient cause of any one phenomenon in nature.

The laws of nature are the rules according to which the effects are produced; but there must be a cause which operates according to these rules. The rules of navigation never navigated a ship. The rules of architecture never built a house. (*EAP* I. 6, p. 46/527a; see also *TAC* 185–6, 209)

What Reid calls the "efficient cause" is, for him, identical to the entity endowed with the "active power" to produce a particular effect and that exerted itself to produce it. It is important to distinguish between active powers and what we might call "capacities" or "dispositions". Active powers and capacities are both qualities of entities by virtue of which they engage in changes. However, if the changes they engage in are changes

---

[4] Reid suggests this term when he writes: "[T]here is [a] meaning of the word cause, which is so well authorized by custom, that we cannot always avoid using it, and I think we may call it the physical sense; as when we say that heat is the cause that turns water into vapour, and cold the cause that freezes it into ice. A cause, in this sense, means only something which, by the laws of nature, the effect always follows" (*COR* 95, p. 178). However, there is a way in which the term might mislead: it might appear that physical causes and physical effects must both be physical events. This, however, is not so. A mental event could be subsumable under a law with a physical event, and could, therefore, be its physical cause or physical effect.

with respect to which they are active, then the relevant quality is an active power; if passive, then the quality is merely a capacity or disposition.[5]

The concept of active power, and, accordingly, the concept of efficient causation, is elusive. Reid notes that our conceptions of power are irremediably relative—our thoughts about a power are always mediated by thoughts about those changes that are due to it—yet they provide no "less fit materials for accurate reasoning" (*EAP* I. 1, 9/514*a*) than do conceptions that are not relative. However, since the same could be said about our conceptions of capacities or dispositions—we conceive of the sugar's capacity to dissolve, for instance, by way of a thought about dissolution—this point by itself does not help us to understand what is meant by "active power". Perhaps, in the end, we can learn more about what Reid takes active power to be through examination of the claims and arguments that he offers with regard to efficient causes, than we can by flat speculation about the notion. Still, metaphors, while limited in the illumination they provide, can be helpful here: power is the quality possessed by the source from which change flows in something like the way in which the source of the river is the place from which its flow emanates. Power, we might say, is the quality possessed by the "buck-stopper" in the regressive search for the ultimate cause of a particular event. The efficient cause of the event is that entity that can be thought of as the originator of the sequence of changes leading to the event; power is the quality that entity possesses by virtue of which it has this status.

Given the distinction between physical and efficient causation, we can identify four grand and incompatible pictures that one might have of the structure of the world underlying observable change. We might hold, first, that there are no efficient causes; genuine powers are nowhere to be found. Reid sometimes attributes this view to Hume (cf. *EIP* VI. 6, p. 500) and, given the darkness that surrounds the notion of active power, there is much to be said for this position. At the other extreme, we might hold that efficient causes are ubiquitous; we might hold, that is, that the ordinary objects that we see and feel—sticks and stones, plants and fish, and our fellow human beings—are efficient causes, in addition to entities like angels and God that lie beyond the sphere of our senses. Between these two extremes lie (at least) two intermediate positions. According to one,

---

[5] The power–capacity distinction is the same as the traditional distinction between active and passive power. Reid, however, objects to the usage of the term "passive power"—"[P]assive power is no power at all" (*EAP* I. 3, p. 23/519*a*)—and so it is better, for our purposes, to avoid the term.

only God is an efficient cause (a view held by Malebranche[6]), and according to another the only efficient causes are God, human beings and other entities endowed with minds, such as angels (if there are any such entities[7]). Reid accepts the last of these views; only entities at the level of human beings, and above that level in the Great Chain of Being, are capable of being efficient causes.

Reid took the postulation of active powers, and an account of their distribution and nature, to be part of what a complete Newtonian science produces. Far from implying Necessitarianism, as Priestley claims, the methods of Newton help us to see, Reid thinks, that there is more involved in human action than can be accounted for under a Necessitarian model of the agent. We are not, he thinks, merely cogs in the great machine, or arenas in which events unfold; rather, we are endowed with active power, a quality that is discovered by the Newtonian as that which must underlie all observable, law-governed change.

The central tenet of Reid's theory of action, then, can be stated very simply: *The actions of an agent are all and only those events of which the agent is the efficient cause.* This book is spent elucidating and evaluating this claim and its implications. Chapters 1 and 2 examine the arguments Reid offers for the claim that any object endowed with active power, any efficient cause, must also have both will and understanding. If these arguments succeed, then Reid has shown that any picture of the world in which ordinary, mindless objects are thought to have powers is mistaken. Chapter 3 is spent examining Reid's grounds for believing that there must be an efficient cause of every change to be found in nature. Although Reid thinks

---

[6] For instance, Malebranche writes, "It is clear that no body, large or small, has the power to move itself. A mountain, a house, a rock, a grain of sand, in short, the tiniest or largest body conceivable does not have the power to move itself...[W]hen we examine our idea of all finite minds, we do not see any necessary connection between their will and the motion of any body whatsoever. On the contrary, we see that there is none and that there can be none. We must therefore also conclude...that there is absolutely no mind created that can move a body as a true or principal cause, just as it has been said that no body could move itself. But when one thinks about the idea of God...one knows there is such a connection between His will and the motion of all bodies, that it is impossible to conceive that He wills a body to be moved and that this body not be moved. We must therefore say that only His will can move bodies" (Nicolas Malebranche, *The Search after Truth*, tr. and ed. T. Lennon (Cambridge: Cambridge University Press, 1997), 448).

[7] Reid consistently expresses agnosticism about the question of whether or not there are any such "subordinate" causes (cf. *EAP* IV. 3, p. 278/606b; *TAC* 222). For our purposes, however, what is important is that Reid's position differs from that of Malebranche in his belief that human beings are among the entities endowed with active power.

that we believe this without the aid of any argument, it is suggested that he is also committed to the claim on the grounds that there is a constitutive link between end-directedness and power; a world lacking in entities with power would also be lacking in any events that are genuinely directed towards ends. Thus, the first three chapters of the book discuss the arguments on the basis of which Reid rejects the two extreme positions regarding the distribution of active power: the position according to which efficient causes are as common as objects themselves, and the position according to which there are no efficient causes at all.

Chapter 4 examines the link between end-directedness and power, and in the process looks at one of the ways in which Reid uses his conception of efficient cause in order to argue that human beings are the efficient causes of their conduct. The argument rests on drawing a connection between planned conduct and efficiently caused conduct, a connection that, it is argued, is intertwined with Reid's conception of character traits. Chapters 5 and 6 turn to Reid's views regarding the role of motives in the etiology of action. While Reid does not offer a substantive, positive account of the influence of motives on the actions performed for their sake, he offers a collection of powerful and provocative arguments against the appealing view that motivational influence is a species of causal influence. Chapter 5 looks at his argument against the claim that motives influence behavior in the way in which efficient causes influence their effects; Chapter 6 looks at his arguments against the claim that motivational influence is a form of physical-causal influence, a claim that underlies most naturalistic theories of action. Chapters 4, 5, and 6, then, explore the contours of Reid's view of end-directed behavior. In the conclusion to the book, the view of efficient causation and motivated action developed in the preceding chapters is used to address the question of whether or not, or in what sense, Reid holds an "agent-causalist" position: a position according to which there is a basic causal relation between agents and events, instantiated in every free action, and not reducible to causal relations obtaining only among events. Ultimately, it is argued that Reid is an agent-causalist but not for the reasons, or in the sense in which, some contemporary philosophers are agent-causalists.

The picture of Reid's view of action and efficient causation offered in this book is of a fundamentally teleological conception both of human action and of natural change. A philosopher who holds that the possibility of law-like change requires that the world be populated with entities endowed with powers is not thereby committed to the claim that wherever there is law-like change there is purpose or intent. But Reid is committed to this claim. He thinks that behind the order discovered and described by natural science there must be entities who aim at the production of that order. Change in nature is, for Reid, always end-directed; things happen because some agent intends that they should.[8] The arguments to be discussed in Chapters 1–3, then, are intended to defend this teleological view of natural change.[9] Reid's arguments for the claim that human beings are endowed with active power, and his accompanying arguments for the claim that to act on a motive, to act for the sake of an end, is not to be caused to act—the arguments to be discussed in Chapters 4–6—amount to an argument for a fundamentally teleological conception of human action. Action, which is the manifestation of one's power, is essentially and irreducibly end-directed behavior.

It is important to distinguish the kind of teleology that Reid, following the Baconian and Newtonian tradition in natural science, rejects from the kind that he takes to be an essential element in all natural change and in all human action. Teleological explanations involve at least the following two elements: they identify the explanandum as a means to the end cited in the explanans, and they assert that some object or agent has the end that the explanans cites. So, for instance, to answer the question, "Why does food digest in the human stomach?" by saying "To spread nutrients through the body" is to assert two things: (1) digestion is a necessary means to the spread of nutrients, and (2) something aims at the spread of nutrients; something, that is, has the spread of nutrients as its end. Neither element is sufficient for explanation by itself: unless something aims at the spread of nutrients, the fact that digestion is a necessary means to that spread does not explain why digestion comes to pass; and, the fact that something aims at the spread of nutrients does not explain why digestion comes to pass unless digestion serves that end.

A general requirement of any explanation, whether or not it is teleological, is that the conditions claimed to obtain in the explanation are distinct from those in need of explanation; otherwise, the explanation explains the puzzling thing by telling us what we already knew when we expressed our

---

[8] Reid is not thereby committed to the view often attributed to Malebranche, according to which each and every event in nature is brought about by a specific intention on God's part favoring that very event. God might intend a particular event only indirectly by intending the law under which the event falls.

[9] This position fits snugly with Reid's "Providentialist Naturalism" discussed by Derek Brookes in his introduction to Reid's *Inquiry*. Cf. pp. ix, xxi–xxiii.

puzzlement in the form of a why-question—namely that the puzzling thing is so. The Baconian tradition objected to teleological explanations on the grounds that all such explanations violate this requirement.[10] Teleological explanations were characterized by the tradition to be little better than appeals to qualities like "dormitive virtues", appeals that were satirized famously by Molière.[11] The question, "Why does opium make people sleep?" is answered by asserting that opium aims at making us sleep; that's what it is to have the dormitive virtue. The problem is that opium has that end if and only if it makes us sleep; hence the explanans isn't sufficiently independent from the explanandum to constitute an adequate explanation. Because it violates this requirement of independence, the purported explanation is vacuous. In this case, the directedness towards the end appealed to in the explanation—the having of the end of making us sleep—is clearly not independent from the events to be explained, for it is identical to them. We might extend the problem even to cases in which the explanandum is merely a means to the end identified in the explanans, but different from it. If an object or agent has the end of spreading nutrients only if it engages in digestion, then the second element of the teleological explanation—that something has the end in question—can be present only if the explanation violates the requirement of independence.

Why, however, can't the having of an end be understood to be a quality—a basic quality of end-directedness—distinct from the adoption of means to that end? If it could be so understood, then teleological explanations could be acquitted of the charge of vacuity. In fact, entities like "substantial forms" were intended by the Aristotelian scholastics to be distinct from any set of behaviors explained by appeal to them; they were ontologically distinct, it was claimed, from the qualities for which they accounted. The traditional problem with qualities like "substantial forms", however, is that our only conception of them is by way of the very qualities that they are meant to explain. When asked what it is to have the end of spreading nutrients (and the more fundamental end of maintaining bodily persistence), one can only say, "Well, it is to have a quality that drives you to do things like

---

[10] Cf. Thomas Hobbes, *Leviathan* (Indianapolis: Hackett Publishing, 1994), IV. 46; Locke, *Essay Concerning Human Understanding*, II. XXI. 20.

[11] A hypochondriac, believing himself to be engaged in a ceremony in which he will be made a doctor, recites the following verse: "*Mihi by docto Doctore / Demandatur causam et rationem quare / Opium facit dormire: / To which respondeo / Quia est in eo / Virtus dormitiva / Cuius est natura / Sensus stupefire.*" (Molière, "The Imaginary Invalid", in *The Misanthrope and Other Plays*, tr. D. M. Frame (New York: Signet Classics, 1968), p. 503.)

engage in digestion, and other behaviors which serve that end." So, even if we admit that the quality of having the end is a different quality from adopting the means, and thus rescue teleological explanation from the problem of non-independence, we are at a loss to provide any definition of end-directedness independently of the adoption of means. The insistence that there is such a quality, different in itself from the adoption of means, seems to be a metaphysical indulgence, an assertion of the existence of a quality that is needed to fill a gap in explanations, but which we have no independent reason to believe to exist.

In all of this, Reid is orthodox. He describes the Aristotelian doctrine of substantial forms, for instance, as an "absurd fiction" (*EIP* II. 17, p. 207), and clearly holds that such qualities are suspect. But then what are we to make of Reid's view to the effect that all changes in nature and all human behaviors are end-directed? That view implies that a fully explanatory account of any phenomenon would have to be teleological. How can a philosopher hold such a position and, at the same time, accept the tradition's grounds for rejecting teleological explanation?

The answer is that Reid thinks that he has independent reasons for believing that a certain class of qualities of end-directedness do exist, despite the fact that they cannot be conceptualized independently of the adoption of means to the end in question. In particular, he thinks that we know that we have certain intentions; and because we know that there are other minds, we know also that those other minds have intentions as well. This doesn't mean that we could define what it is to have such intentions without making reference to the very behaviors that appeals to intention are meant to explain, but only that we know that we have intentions for reasons independent of any explanatory role that we wish them to play. To have an intention is to be directed towards a particular end, and so it is to have a quality much like a dormitive virtue or substantial form, with this difference: dormitive virtues and substantial forms are supposedly possessed by mindless entities like opium, while intentions are possessed only by minds. What makes a substantial form an "absurd fiction"? Reid thinks that qualities like substantial forms are absurd because *to appeal to them is to ascribe purposes to things that are incapable of thinking about the ends at which they presumably strive*.[12] (Chapters 1 and 2, discussing Reid's arguments for

[12] One piece of evidence for this derives from the fact that Reid explains the practice of using the word "cause" to apply not just to efficient causes, or things genuinely endowed with active power, but also to physical causes, by insisting that that practice is a remnant of the tendency to

the claim that power requires a mind, explain Reid's reasons for holding this view.) But there is no similar absurdity to be found in intention. Our minds are the sorts of things that can have intentions or purposes; they are the sorts of things that can, in their nature, *aim*. So, the sort of teleology that Reid accepts is the sort that involves ascription of basic qualties of end-directedness—qualities that have an existence independent from the behaviors they are invoked to explain—but ascribes such qualities only to creatures with minds; the sort that he rejects is the sort that ascribes such qualities even to things lacking the capacity for thought.

In Reid's theory of action—his view that there is an identity between human actions and behaviors of which human beings are the efficient causes—a number of central tenets of his philosophical thought meet. His theory of action is a product of his recognition of both the attractions and the limitations of the "covering law" model of scientific explanation. It is, relatedly, a product of his belief that, for all its virtues, the Humean equation between causation and subsumption under law is limited and fails to reach the fundamental metaphysical facts underlying natural change. And, perhaps most importantly, his theory of action is also a product of his belief that the mind is the only arena in which legitimate and irreducible properties can be found from which all end-directedness springs. This book is an effort to elucidate and critically evaluate the portrait of human agency that emerges from this confluence of views.

ascribe life and intelligence to physical causes (cf. *EAP* IV. 3). In other words, before we know that things like the sun do not have minds, they seem to be legitimate contenders to be efficient causes; once we learn, however, that they lack minds, we recognize that they cannot be the real, efficient causes of things. Since the discovery that the sun lacks a mind disqualifies it from possession of the power to melt wax only if possession of that power requires a mind, Reid must think that what makes appeal to intention metaphysically superior to appeal to the likes of dormitive virtues is that the former necessarily ascribes power only to a thing with a mind.

1

From Power to Mind: An Argument from the Power to Exert

Reid states the first of his arguments for the claim that where there is active power there is also will and understanding as follows:

[I]f we had not will, and that degree of understanding which will necessarily implies, we could exert no active power, and consequently could have none: for power that cannot be exerted is no power. It follows also, that the active power, of which only we can have any distinct conception, can be only in beings that have understanding and will.   (*EAP* I. 5, p. 35/523*a*)

Reid appears to be offering the following argument:

(1.1) S has a power only if S has the power to exert it.[1]
(1.2) S has the power to exert only if S has a will.

---

[1] Some might balk at this gloss on Reid's remark that "power that cannot be exerted is no power" on the grounds that it commits Reid to a problematic regress: if the power to act requires the power to exert, and exertion is action, then it also requires the power to exert one's power to exert, and the power to exert one's power to exert one's power to exert, and so on. In order to avoid this, we might, instead, say that what Reid is after should be summarized as follows: "S has a power only if S can exert it". The question, then, is what is meant by "can" here. If "can" refers to a capacity or disposition to exert, then the force of Reid's argument will be lost: as will become clear in discussion of premise (1.2), there is no reason to think that the *capacity* to exert requires a will, even though there may be reason to think the power to exert does. On the other hand, if "can" refers to a power to exert, then the proposed alternative interpretation is not an alternative at all. Better, I think, is to try to address the worries about regress head on, in the face of the recognition that Reid does indeed hold (1.1). This is attempted in the Conclusion of this book.

(1.3) S has a will only if S has an understanding.

∴ S has power only if S has a will and an understanding.

Each of the premises in this argument deserves discussion.

Premise (1.1): S Has a Power Only if S has the Power to Exert it

Reid supports premise (1.1) by saying that "power that cannot be exerted is no power". This, however, simply amounts to the reassertion of premise (1.1). Still, we might motivate premise (1.1) by appeal to Reid's critical remarks concerning the conception of power offered by Hobbes and taken up by the compatibilist tradition following him. Under Reid's interpretation, Hobbes defines power as follows:

> *Hobbesian Power:* S has a power to A *if and only if* if S chooses to A, then S As.[2]

The standard criticism of the account appeals to an intuition to the effect that A cannot be in the agent's power if the choice to A is not also within his power.[3] Since the Hobbesian account does not require that the choice be within the agent's power, the standard criticism seems to show that the account is in conflict with intuition. The standard criticism, then, is vulnerable to the standard response to appeals to intuition: simply deny the intuition. That is, the defender of the Hobbesian account of power can simply dismiss the intuition as a confusion to which we are subject largely because of our pre-theoretic failure to appreciate the nature of power.

Reid offers a variant of the standard criticism of the Hobbesian account of power: "[T]o say that what depends upon the will is in a man's power, but the will is not in his power, is to say that the end is in his power, but the means necessary to that end are not in his power, which is a contradiction"

---

[2] For instance, Hobbes writes: "[H]e is free to do a thing, that may do it if he have the will to do it, and may forbear, if he have the will to forbear" ("Of Liberty and Necessity", *English Works of Thomas Hobbes*, iv. 240). See also *EAP* IV. 1, p. 265/602b.

[3] The criticism was standard even in Hobbes's time, and it remains standard today. Consider Hobbes's objector, Bishop Bramhall: "If the will have no power over itself, the man is no more free than a staff in a man's hand" ("A Defense of True Liberty" in *Hobbes and Bramhall on Liberty and Necessity*, ed. V. Chappell (Cambridge: Cambridge University Press, 1999), 44). For a recent statement of the same objection, consider Roderick Chisholm: "If the man could not have chosen to do otherwise, then he would not have done otherwise—*even if* he was such that, if he *had* chosen to do otherwise, then he would have done otherwise" ("Human Freedom and the Self", in G. Watson (ed.), *Free Will* (Oxford: Oxford University Press, 1982), 27).

(*EAP* IV. 1, p. 266/602b). Reid's objection to the Hobbesian account of power seems, at first glance anyway, more promising than the standard criticism because it avoids an explicit appeal to intuition with regard to what is and is not in one's power. Instead, Reid appeals to an attractive general principle that he thinks no one would want to deny:

> *Means–End Power Transference*: If M is a necessary means to E, and S has the power to E, then S has the power to M.

There are two questions to answer. First, is this principle true? And, second, if it is true, can it be supported without flat appeal to intuition of the sort employed in the standard criticism?

To answer these questions, consider, first, the following conception of "necessary means":

> *Weak Conception*: Event M is a necessary means to event E *if and only if* E cannot occur unless M occurs.

Under the weak conception, the drying of a wet match is a necessary means to its lighting (assuming that the word "cannot" is being used in the sense of nomic, rather than logical necessity). But an agent might have the power to light the wet match an hour from now, when it will be dry, despite the fact that he lacks the power to dry the match. It might be that he need do nothing at all to see to it that the match is dry; it will dry all by itself, or just because of the lucky fact that the rain has stopped and the sun is out. If so, then the fact that the agent happens to lack the power to do anything that would dry the match—he has no 350° oven handy, for instance—does not undermine his power to light it. The point is that, however the match comes to be dry, its drying needn't be thought to spring from an exercise of the agent's active power. Assuming that every event is efficiently caused (a claim to be discussed in Chapter 3), in such a case, the efficient cause behind the physical cause–effect connection resulting in the dry match is not the agent but, instead, whatever the efficient cause is of normal natural phenomena. So, under the weak conception of necessary means, Reid's principle of Means–End Power Transference is false.

Reid can't have the weak conception of necessary means in mind. In another context, Reid offers the following example:

[H]e who maliciously intends to shoot his neighbor dead, and voluntarily does it, is undoubtedly the cause of his death, though he did no more to occasion it than to draw the trigger of the gun. He neither gave to the ball its velocity, nor to the powder its expansive force, nor to the flint and steel the power to strike fire; but he knew what he did must be followed by the man's death, and did it with that intention; and therefore he is justly chargeable with the murder. (*EAP* I. 7, p. 51/528*b*)

Since the neighbor can't be killed if, for instance, the powder doesn't have a tendency to expand when lit, the possession of that tendency would count as a necessary means to the killing, under the weak conception of necessary means. It would follow from the Means–End Power Transference principle that the man lacked the power to kill his neighbor since he lacks the power to make the powder expand when lit. But if this were so, Reid would deny that the man is "justly chargeable" with the murder. Reid says that "We can never conceive that a man's duty goes beyond his power" (*EAP* I. 5, p. 38/524*a*), and so he must hold that no one can be held responsible for an event that it was not in his power to bring about. But since Reid thinks that the man is "justly chargeable" his remarks here commit him to denying either the principle of Means–End Power Transference, or else the weak conception of necessary means. He seems more likely to be denying the latter, given that he explicitly offers the former.

However, in at least one place, Reid seems to invoke the weak conception of necessary means while, in the same breath, making a remark that is flatly inconsistent with the principle of Means–End Power Transference. He writes,

There are many things necessary to be done for our preservation, which, even when we will to do, we know not the means by which they must be done.

A man knows that he must swallow his food before it can nourish him. But this action requires the cooperation of many nerves and muscles, of which he knows nothing; and if it were to be directed solely by his understanding and will, he would starve before he learned how to perform it. (*EAP* III. 1. ii, pp. 105–6/547*a*)

Presumably, the man has the power to nourish himself, but lacks the power to contract the needed muscles since he doesn't know what muscles need to be contracted.[4] But Reid asserts here that the contraction of muscles is

---

[4] At least, the man lacks the power to contract the needed muscles if a particular doctrine regarding the epistemic conditions for the possession of an ability is true. The doctrine in question is this: you lack the power to A if you don't know what state of affairs would need to obtain for it to be true that you A. In this formulation, it is left open exactly what you need to know in order to have this knowledge, and it is clear that the knowledge required is sensitive to the description of the act. In the case under consideration, the man clearly does not know enough about the relevant state of affairs to have the relevant ability. The man might not know, even, that he has muscles in his throat, much less which ones are contracted, and in which order, when

the "means by which [the swallowing] must be done". It seems to follow, then, that Reid is denying the Means–End Power Transference principle. Better, however, is to take Reid to be noticing, although a bit dimly, that the Means–End Power Transference principle is inconsistent with the weak conception of necessary means. What this implies is that he must have some other notion of necessary means in mind when he asserts that principle in his attack on the Hobbesian account of power.

Notice that if the principle of Means–End Power Transference is true, then possession of the power to M is one of the necessary conditions of E's occurrence. But surely the power to E does not require *power over* the possession of the power to M. To say that it did would be to take the first step towards regress: wouldn't the power to E also require the power to possess the power to possess the power to M? What this shows is that acceptance of the principle of Means–End Power Transference requires denying the claim that every necessary condition for the occurrence of what is in your power is also in your power. Since the weak conception of necessary means makes no distinction between the necessary means to a particular event's occurrence and any other necessary condition, those who accept the principle of Means–End Power Transference must reject the weak conception of necessary means. However, there do seem to be necessary conditions for the occurrence of a particular event over which one must have power in order to have power over the event. The thought that, at least, the necessary *means* to the occurrence of a particular event must be in one's power, if the event is to be in one's power, is one way of trying to make good on that thought by distinguishing the necessary conditions over which one needs to have power from those necessary conditions over which one need not have power in order to have power over the event for which they are necessary. The difficulty comes in identifying what makes a particular event a necessary means for another, as opposed to a merely necessary condition, and the weak conception is too weak.

One might think that the crucial difference between necessary means and other necessary conditions is that the necessary means are those necessary conditions that the agent can't count on obtaining on their own, and so the agent must plan to do what is necessary to make sure they obtain. This is to say that we might think that necessary means are all of them actions of the relevant agent, and that is what distinguishes them from

he swallows. So, although he has the ability to swallow, he doesn't have the ability to perform the act of contracting the relevant muscles, despite the fact that swallowing and contracting the relevant muscles are the same event under different descriptions.

other necessary conditions. Accordingly, Reid might be employing a stronger, and more plausible, conception of "necessary means":

> *Strong Conception:* M is agent S's necessary means to E *if and only if* (1) E cannot occur unless M occurs, and (2) M is an action of S's.

Here, the term "action" is being used to demarcate those events that are expressions of a particular person's active power from those that are not; an event is S's action just in case it is the product, in some sense, of S's active power.

Under the strong conception of "necessary means", Reid's principle is true. After all, M's occurrence is the occurrence of something with respect to which S is active, and so S would have to have the power to M if M is to occur. Since E's occurrence requires M, it also requires that S have the power to M. Thus we have a connection between E's occurrence and the power to M. Since this is not yet a connection between the power to bring about E and the power to M, but only a connection between E's *occurrence* and the power to M, we have not yet provided the connection between the power to E and the power to M asserted by the principle of Means–End Power Transference. But that final connection can be made by invoking the following principle that, I think, no one would wish to reject:

> (*) If, at time t_0, S has the power to A at t_1 then all those conditions necessary for A's occurrence (other than S's exertion of his power) hold at t_1.[5]

If we assume that M is a necessary means to E in the strong sense of "necessary means", then M's occurrence is a necessary condition for E's occurrence (clause (1) of the strong conception of necessary means) and M is an action (clause (2) of the strong conception of necessary means). However, if M is an action, it is an expression of the agent's active power, and thus S's power to M is a necessary condition of M's occurrence. But since M's occurrence is a necessary condition of E's occurrence, it follows that S's power to M is a necessary condition for E's occurrence. But now imagine that S has the power to E. It follows from (*) that all the necessary conditions for E's occurrence, including the having of the power to M by S, will be in place at the needed time. So, given (*), if an agent has the power

---

[5] The conditions need not hold at t_0. I could have the power now to watch the sunrise tomorrow morning despite the fact that my present position on the earth precludes my watching the sunrise now.

to E he also has the power to M. That is, Reid's Means–End Power Transference principle follows.

However, the principle of Means–End Power Transference can only be employed to object to the Hobbesian analysis of power if the Hobbesian agrees that choices are actions. Otherwise, clause (2) of the strong conception of necessary means won't hold when M is the choice and E is the action, and so the choice would not count as the necessary means to the action. But for the Hobbesian to agree that choices are actions—are expressive of active power—is already to accept that an agent who has the power to act has the power to choose. After all, if choices are actions, then a necessary condition for the occurrence of a choice is power on the part of the agent whose choice it is. This is to say that, if Reid is employing the strong conception of necessary means, then his objection to Hobbesian power ultimately involves the same flat appeal to intuition involved in the standard criticism.

It seems, then, that one way or another what really fuels Reid's objection to the Hobbesian conception of power is the view that exertions of power are themselves actions. This claim is, itself, thought to be a deliverance of introspection. We are supposed to be conscious of the fact that our exertions of power are events with respect to which we are active; they wear their activity on their face. To see this, note first that Reid favors Locke's passing explanation for the origin of our idea of active power: that it is acquired through reflection on our capacity to move our bodies and direct our thoughts (*Essay Concerning Human Understanding*, II. XXI. 4). Reid writes, "[O]f the manner in which a cause may exert its active power, we can have no conception but from consciousness of the manner in which our own active power is exerted" (*EAP* I. 5, p. 36/523b). Reid suggests that this is how we are able to know that we ourselves are the efficient causes of our own actions, while we are never able to know of natural events what particular thing is the efficient cause of them. Even though we are able to know that each event in nature has some efficient cause, unless we know what being exerted its power to produce the event, we cannot know what being was the efficient cause:

When I observe a plant growing from its seed to maturity, I know that there must be a cause that has power to produce this effect. But I see neither the cause nor the manner of its operation.

But in certain motions of my body, and directions of my thought, I know, not only that there must be a cause that has power to produce these effects, but that I am that cause; and I am conscious of what I do in order to the production of them. (*EAP* I. 5, p. 36/523b)

The attribution of an event such as a bodily movement to oneself is a derived attribution: we attribute such events to ourselves because we attribute to ourselves exertions of power to produce the events in question. However, if we were to attribute exertions of power to ourselves on the same grounds—because they spring from further exertions of power—then regress would loom. If Reid is to avoid regress, then, the recognition of an exertion of one's power as one's own action is not derived but direct. In being conscious of our exertions of power we are at once also conscious of the fact that they are the products of power; we are conscious, that is, that they are *exertions* and, as such, are expressions of our activity.[6] Events that follow on these efforts are also events with respect to which we are active, but not by virtue of intrinsic features immediately accessible to consciousness, but, instead, by virtue of their relationship to exertions of power. The following passage represents a statement of the view: "Every man is led by nature to attribute to himself the free determinations of his own will, and to believe those events to be in his power which depend upon his will" (*EAP* I. 5, p. 37/524a). To be "led by nature" to accept a proposition is to accept the proposition independently of any either deductive or inductive epistemic support that might be given to it. (For instance, "first principles" are, for Reid, those that we are led by nature to accept.) The claim of this passage, then, is that we attribute our volitions to ourselves directly, and not by virtue of, or on the basis of, the attribution to ourselves of something else from which they spring. Where bodily movements that spring from our efforts are mediate expressions of power—we attribute them to ourselves only because they spring from volitions that we attribute to ourselves—the efforts themselves are the immediate expressions of power.

Reid accepts, then, the following position: every act, other than an exertion of power, inherits its status as an act from some other act to which it is (probably nomically) related. The act from which it inherits its act status, in turn, is either a basic act, or it too inherits its act status from some other act. The basic acts are exertions of power: they are acts not by virtue of the relation they bear to some other act, but by virtue of features they possess that are immediately accessible to consciousness.[7] To know if a bodily

---

[6] Locke had a different, but related view. For discussion, see Gideon Yaffe, *Liberty Worth the Name: Locke on Free Agency* (Princeton: Princeton University Press, 2000), esp. 112–17.

[7] Reid would probably not accept this precise formulation since he would deny that a volition is the sort of thing that can have properties. Better, perhaps, is to say that volitions consist, in part, in properties of the agent that are immediately accessible to consciousness, and by virtue of which the agent is active with respect to the volition.

movement is an action, or merely a reflex, say, we need to examine the mental states from which it springs; if they are actions, it is too. However, to know if an exertion of power is an action we need only examine the exertion of power itself; it wears its activity on its face.

How does this picture help to support premise (1.1)? The idea might be that an event like a bodily movement, say, will not just occur if one wills it, but it will also be *an action*. Hence, if it is possible for it to come about, it must be possible for the basic act from which it inherits its status as action to come about; that is, it must be possible for the exertion of power to come about. But since the exertion is necessarily an act, it cannot spring from a passive disposition on the part of the agent, but only from an active power. Hence it follows that if the agent has the power to act in a certain way, the agent also has the power to exert that power. Put more formally, Reid could be construed as accepting the following argument for premise (1.1):

(1.1i) If S has the power to A, then it is possible that S As.
(1.1ii) If it is possible that S As, then it is possible that S engages in a basic act by virtue of which A is an action.
(1.1iii) If it is possible that S engages in a basic act, then S has the power to engage in that basic act.
(1.1iv) Any basic act by virtue of which A is an action is an exertion of the power to A.[8]
∴ If S has the power to A, then S has the power to exert that power.

One remarkable fact about this argument is that it is consistent with the Hobbesian conception of every power to act other than the power to exert, for only basic acts are such that the mere possibility of performing one entails possession of the power to perform it. The Hobbesian can admit that in order to have the power to, say, touch my nose it must be possible for me to will to touch my nose; what the Hobbesian cannot admit is that that possibility requires the power to will to touch my nose.[9] Given,

---

[8] The above reflection on the principle of Means–End Power Transference reveals Reid's commitment to this premise.

[9] One might think that those who endorse the Hobbesian conception of power with respect to acts other than exertions of power would reject premise (1.1i). Whether or not this is so, however, depends on how the term "possible" is interpreted. Most compatibilists would accept that it is possible that an agent should exert his power, and so it is possible that he should act, even if he did not exert his power and could not have done so given the laws and the past. This is to interpret the term "possible" here as the same as either "there is a possible world that shares the laws with the actual world (but might have a different past) such that" or "there is a possible world that shares the past with the actual world (but might have different laws) such that",

then, that the argument only contradicts the Hobbesian conception of the power to exert, it is not as surprising as it might at first appear to find Reid making remarks that seem on their face to be straightforward endorsements of that conception of power: "[I]t is self-evident, that nothing is in our power that is not subject to our will" (*EAP* I. 5, p. 37/524*a*). And, more clearly, "We can never conceive that a man's . . . power goes beyond what depends upon his will" (*EAP* I. 5, p. 38/524*a*). Notice that in these remarks Reid does not say that it is sufficient for the possession of every power, including the power to exert, that the conditional "If S exerts, he acts" is true. Rather he uses the terminology of "dependence" on the will. Even exertions of power, since they will turn out to be all of them volitions, are dependent on the will; however, they are dependent on the will in a sense importantly different from the sense in which all other acts in an agent's power are dependent on his will.[10] Exertions are not in an agent's power by virtue of the fact that they will occur should the agent exert himself to bring them about; but, nonetheless, they would not occur were the agent not invested with a will; and, further, they are in an agent's power because of the relation they bear *to* the agent's power. As is typical of Reid, he objects not to the letter of the conceptual analyses offered by the likes of Hobbes, Locke, Berkeley, and Hume; he accepts the equation between what is in our power and what is dependent on our will. He objects, instead, to the implications that those philosophers took to follow from their conceptual analyses, and in particular to the view that the only sense in which an act can be dependent on the will is that it be such as to follow from an *exercise* of will (the view labeled above as "the Hobbesian conception of power"). The Hobbesian conception of power is right, as far as it goes, but the compatibilists who accept it draw the unfortunate (as Reid sees it) conclusion that we can be passive with respect to our exertions of power and can, therefore, be invested with powers by virtue of being the conduit of forces that originate elsewhere, or nowhere at all. That is, they think that we can be invested with active powers in virtue of the possession

---

rather than interpreting it to mean "there is a possible world that shares both the laws and the past with the actual world such that". If "possible" is interpreted in this last sense, then the Hobbesian would reject premise (1.1i).

[10] Reid makes essentially this point when he writes: "In many propositions which we express universally, there is an exception necessarily implied, and therefore always understood. Thus when we say that all things depend upon God, God himself is necessarily excepted. In like manner, when we say, that all that is in our power depends upon the will, the will itself is necessarily excepted; for if the will be not, nothing else can be in our power" (*EAP* IV. 1, p. 266/602*b*).

of passive dispositions to choose, while Reid thinks that all choices are acts and so there are no passive dispositions to choose. Instead, the power to act must be rooted, ultimately, in the active power to exert.

Premise (1.2): S Has the Power to Exert Only if S has a Will

Reid explicitly offers an independent argument for premise (1.2). He writes,

> From the consciousness of our own activity, seems to be derived, not only the clearest, but the only conception we can form of activity, or the exertion of active power.
> As I am unable to form a notion of any intellectual power different in kind from those I possess, the same holds with respect to active power. (*EAP* I. 5, p. 36/523b)

A bit earlier, Reid associates the exertion of power in ourselves with willing, or volition. With approval, he summarizes a passage from Locke:[11]

> According to Mr. Locke, therefore, the only clear notion or idea we have of active power, is taken from the power which we find in ourselves to give certain motions to our bodies, or a certain direction to our thoughts; and this power in ourselves can be brought into action only by willing or volition. (*EAP* I. 5, p. 35/523a)

When these two passages are put together, Reid seems to be offering the following argument for premise (1.2):

(1.2i) Our only conception of exertion derives from the consciousness of our own exertions.

(1.2ii) All of our own exertions are volitions.

(1.2iii) We are unable to conceive of intellectual powers different in kind from those we possess.

(1.2iv) An active power would be different in kind from those we possess if the exertion of it did not consist in volition.

(1.2v) There are no active powers different in kind from those of which we are able to conceive.

∴ All exertions of active power are volitions.[12]

---

[11] *Essay Concerning Human Understanding*, II. XXI. 4–5.

[12] In at least one place, Reid makes a remark that seems to contradict this conclusion. He writes: "There is evidently an Active Power exerted both by Animals and Vegetables. Active Power implies an active agent, and inert Matter can be no such Agent" (*TAC* 229). This remark is made as part of an argument to the effect that there is something immaterial that "animates"

Premise (1.2) follows immediately from the conclusion of this argument: If all exertions are volitions, then the power to exert is the power to have volitions, that is, the will.

Premises (1.2i), (1.2iv), and (1.2v) are relatively unproblematic. The first is the upshot of a Humean lesson about causation to which Reid refers in various places: power is not observable at all, and exertion is not observable through the senses; all we ever see are constant conjunctions between events. To know whether or not (1.2iv) is true we would need to know more about what makes one intellectual power "different in kind" from another. However, it seems that, if the exertions of two intellectual powers are different in kind, then the two powers, also, are different in kind. Given that volitions are a distinct kind of event, the defining features of which are accessible to consciousness, (1.2iv) follows.

Reid is well-known for rejecting the claim that our capacity for conceiving a state of affairs is a measure of its possibility (cf. *EIP* IV. 4, pp. 327–33), and that rejection might appear to be inconsistent with premise (1.2v). However, what Reid is really concerned to reject is the claim that we cannot conceive an impossible state of affairs; he thinks we can. This, however, is perfectly consistent with the further claim, that Reid never denies, that what we cannot conceive is impossible. That is, he is concerned to reject the claim that conceivability implies possibility, not the converse claim that inconceivability implies impossibility. Reid would probably deny that anything that any particular person finds to be inconceivable is, on those grounds, impossible; after all, lots of parochialisms can undermine one's capacity to conceive of something without indicating anything about the possibility or impossibility of that thing. But even this is consistent with the view that something that *our nature as human beings* excludes us from being able to conceive is impossible. In the argument under consideration, it is our natural incapacity to conceive of active powers different in kind from our own that rules out their existence. Thus, (1.2v) is an instance of the basic methodological assumption (guiding not just Reid, but, in a different form, Hume, as well) that anything of which we are incapable by nature of conceiving does not exist.

Premise (1.2ii) follows from (1.2i), together with the claim, supported by introspection, that all of the exertions of which we are conscious are

plants and animals. However, since Reid holds that plants and animals do not have wills, he must hold that the exertions of their active powers are not volitions. The remark, however, appears in a draft of an essay discussing Priestley's conception of materialism, and was never published. There is reason, then, to deny that it expresses Reid's settled position.

volitions; we never find ourselves trying to do things without willing them. If consciousness, rather than perception, is the only form of awareness of exertions, then we cannot be exerting in ways of which we are not conscious. Something, after all, needs to supply an object to thoughts about exertions; if consciousness is our only capacity for supplying such an object, then we are barred from having thoughts about exertions in ourselves that are not thoughts about exertions of which we are conscious. And if all of the exertions of which we are conscious are volitions, then (1.2ii) is true. However, Reid seems flatly to deny that introspection tells us that all the exertions of which we are conscious are volitions, and seems flatly to deny premise (1.2ii). He writes, "Volition, I think does not admit of degrees. It is complete in itself and incapable of more and less. Exertion on the other hand may be great or small or middling. Therefore, exertion and volition are not the same" (OP 5). However, Reid uses the term "exertion" in (at least) two distinct senses.[13] Notice, first, that it is impossible to see how that to which the term "exertion" refers could admit of degrees when Reid makes claims such as the following:

> All that is necessary to the production of any effect, is power in an efficient cause to produce the effect, and the exertion of that power: for it is a contradiction to say, that the cause has the power to produce the effect, and exerts that power, and yet the effect is not produced. (*EAP* IV. 2, p. 268/603*b*)

If the exertion referred to here admits of degrees, then one would think that more of it would make the effect more likely to occur. However, in that case, it is no contradiction to imagine exertion and power without effect: the agent in such a case simply didn't exert himself enough. Since Reid evidently thinks that exertion and power *necessitate* the relevant effect, exertion cannot admit of degrees any more than necessity can.[14]

---

[13] Paul Hoffman, "Thomas Reid's Notion of Exertion", unpublished manuscript, notes a number of different senses in which Reid uses the term.

[14] Active power, for Reid, also cannot admit of degrees, and for the same reasons (contrary to the view expressed in Ferenc Huoranszki, "Common Sense and the Theory of Human Behavior", in J. Haldane and S. Read (eds.), *The Philosophy of Thomas Reid* (London: Blackwell Publishing, 2003), 113–30 (esp. p. 123)). This may seem to be in conflict with various things Reid says. For instance: "[A]ppetites and passion give an impulse to act and impair liberty, in proportion to their strength" (*EAP* II. 2, p. 75/536*b*). Since liberty is just an active power—power over the determinations of the will—this remark seems to imply that that power, at least, must admit of degrees. However, another remark of Reid's gives us some guidance about how to understand this "degree" talk. He writes: "[Active power] is a quality which may be varied, not only in degree, but also in kind; and we distinguish both the kinds and degrees by the effects which they are able to produce" (*EAP* I. 1, p. 10/514*b*). What this remark implies is that the power to lift a

It seems more likely that in the passage just quoted, in which Reid denies an equation between exertion and volition, he is using the term "exertion" to refer to the feeling of effort, which does admit of degrees. However, the feeling of effort bears no important relation to power in the way that exertion, properly speaking, does. Therefore, it seems most likely that Reid does accept premise (1.2ii) on the grounds of introspection, but uses the term "exertion" somewhat more loosely than he ought to.

In fact, the thought that Reid uses the term "exertion" to refer to the feeling of effort, rather than using it in the strict sense to refer to the manifestation of active power, is given further credence by considering the immediate context in which Reid denies an equation between exertion and volition. Reid's remarks to that effect appear in an essay written very late in Reid's life—after the publication of the *Essays on the Active Powers*—and published for the first time in 2001. At the point at which Reid offers considerations against equating exertion and volition, he is offering an argument for the following claim: "an exertion is something different from a deliberate will to produce the event by that exertion" (OP 3). Reid feels that he needs to argue for that claim in order to vindicate a particular way of explaining how we acquire our conception of power through experience:

[O]ur first exertions are instinctive, without any distinct conception of the event that is to follow, consequently without will to produce that event. And that finding by experience that such exertions are followed by such events, we learn to make the exertion voluntarily and deliberately, as often as we desire to produce the event. And when we know or believe that the event depends upon our exertion, we have the conception of power in ourselves to produce the event.   (OP 3)

Notice that Reid does not suggest that we are active with respect to the events that follow upon our early "instinctive" exertions. The baby, for instance, notices that the hand moves following the instinctive exertion to move it, but there is no reason to think the baby is active with respect to the movement; that is really the upshot of calling such exertions "instinctive".

---

10 lbs weight and the power to lift a 20 lbs weight are not the same power, differing only in degrees. Rather, they are different powers *with respect to actions of the same kind and differing only in degree*. If both a weakling and a body builder are capable of lifting a 5 lbs weight, then they both have that power, period. It would be wrong to say that the weakling has it to a lesser degree than the body builder. The only sense in which the body builder has more power than the weakling is that there are other actions of the same kind, but of greater degree, as that of lifting a 5 lbs weight—such as the act of lifting a 200 lbs weight—which the body builder has and the weakling lacks. Degrees, we might say, are not in the powers, but in the acts over which agents have power.

So what is the instinctive exertion? It seems likely that it is just the feeling of effort, but since it is not accompanied with a conception of the hand's movement, in our example, or a belief that the hand's movement will follow upon the having of the feeling, it is not a genuine exercise of active power. It is only after the baby has acquired such a conception and belief that its exertions become genuine exertions, or manifestations of active power. These genuine exertions are all of them self-consciously aimed efforts to bring about changes, and such self-conscious efforts are, for Reid, all of them volitions. So when Reid distinguishes exertion from volition he is using the term "exertion" to refer to the early feelings of effort that he thinks we must have before we can come to be genuinely active. However, if we reserve the term "exertion" to refer to genuine manifestations of active power, then all our exertions are volitions, and it is that sense that Reid has in mind in premise (1.2ii).

It is not initially clear why Reid should believe premise (1.2iii), the claim that we are unable to conceive of intellectual powers different in kind from those we possess. For one thing, there seem to be some obvious counterexamples: we can conceive of the capacity for echolocation despite the fact that we don't have powers that are like that power in any significant respect. We can respond on Reid's behalf to such examples through reflection on another difficulty with premise (1.2iii): (1.2iii) appears to be in conflict with a claim that Reid makes quite frequently. He claims that certain bits of behavior, like facial expressions, are "natural signs" of intellectual powers (cf. *INQ* 5. 3, p. 60; *EIP* VI. 5, pp. 484–7).[15] That is, we come to have a conception of the intellectual powers of others on observation of their behaviors. The import of calling these behaviors "natural signs" of the intellectual powers is that it amounts to claiming that there is no deductive or inductive inference from those behaviors to belief in the existence of the relevant powers; there is no similarity between the signs (facial expressions, gestures) and what they signify (intellectual powers); nor do we have independent observational access to the intellectual powers of others and find them to be conjoined with certain behaviors. Rather, we simply know their capacities for thought and feeling on observing their behavior. But then why shouldn't it be possible for us to conceive of intellectual powers entirely different from our own that happen to be expressed by the behaviors

---

[15] Essentially the same problem is raised in R. F. Stalley, "Causality and Agency in the Philosophy of Thomas Reid", in M. Dalgarno and E. Matthews (eds.), *The Philosophy of Thomas Reid* (Dordrecht: Kluwer Academic Publishers, 1989), 276–7.

of others? Since there is no fitness relation, or similarity relation, between the behaviors and the powers they signify, there is no reason deriving from the nature of behavior, or the nature of the manner in which we come to know of the intellectual powers of others, to preclude the possibility of behaviors that provide us with a conception of intellectual powers entirely different from our own.

In other places besides his statement of the argument for premise (1.2) Reid does restrict our capacity to conceive of intellectual powers to the capacity to conceive of powers similar to our own. For instance, he writes, "I believe the best reason we can give to prove that other men are living and intelligent, is, that their words and actions indicate *like powers of understanding as we are conscious of in ourselves*" (*EIP* VI. 5, p. 483; my emphasis; see also *EAP* IV. 2, p. 270/604*a*). And, further, it seems that this is what distinguishes the behavioral natural signs of the thoughts, feelings and intellectual powers of others from sensations, the natural signs involved in perception. In the *Inquiry*, Reid divides natural signs into three classes. In all three, the natural sign, N, is conjoined (naturally, without artifice) with that which it signifies, O. In the first class belong those natural signs in which both N and O are accessible to observation and where experience of the conjunction of the two is required in order to recognize that N is a sign of O. Reid describes the second and third class of natural signs as follows:

A second class is that wherein the connection between the sign and thing signified, is not only established by nature, but discovered to us by a natural principle, without reasoning or experience....

A third class of natural signs comprehends those which, though we never before had any notion or conception of the things signified, do suggest it, or conjure it up, as it were, by a natural kind of magic, and at once give us a conception, and create a belief of it. (*INQ* 5. 3, p. 60)

In the second class belong facial expressions, and similar behaviors, that express thoughts, feelings and intellectual powers. In the third class belong sensations that express the qualities of material objects. But why do these two belong in different classes? After all, in both cases we need have no independent access to O in order to conceive of it on encountering N. The answer is that in the case of sensations we have a conception of O on encountering N even if we have never encountered anything *of the same kind* as O; we need never have encountered anything hard in order to conceive of hardness after having a certain tactile sensation. However, in the case of behaviors that express the inner lives of others, we have encountered things of the same sort as those that are expressed by the signs; that is, we have conscious experience of the features of our own inner lives.[16]

We still might ask why it is that we are capable of conceiving of qualities of material objects entirely different in kind from anything of which we are conscious—that, after all, is what happens in perception—and yet we are incapable of conceiving of qualities of other minds that are different in kind from our own. However, the question is analogous to asking why it is that a certain tactile sensation leads us to conceive of the hardness of an object and not its color: the right Reidian answer is that that is simply how we are built. Similarly, Reid is likely to say that it is simply a basic fact about us, not amenable to further explanation, that restricts our conceptions of other minds to powers similar to our own while allowing that we are capable of conceiving of features of bodies entirely different from anything to which we have direct access in consciousness. What other possible explanation could be given?

Still, the motivating idea behind the thought that there is some important asymmetry in our capacity to conceive of the features of material and mental objects might very well have its roots in the familiar thought that mental properties, unlike material properties, are irreducibly subjective. To conceive of a mental property must be to conceive of what it is like to have it; to fail to appreciate the subjective aspect of a mental state is to fail to be thinking of that mental state at all. So, we might say, there is some significant sense in which we cannot conceive of the capacity for echolocation, despite the fact that we are perfectly capable of defining the term. If we accept this attractive view, then it is really no surprise that premise (1.2iii) should be true despite the fact that we are perfectly capable of conceiving of many non-intellectual properties of objects that are entirely different from those we ourselves possess. To conceive of an intellectual power of another creature is to put yourself in the place of a thing that has that power; it is to imagine "what it's like" to have a certain sort of mind. But if the mental is irremediably subjective, then this imaginative exercise can only be built on our own subjective experience.

There is some, albeit indirect, evidence to suggest that Reid's argument for premise (1.2) is rooted in thoughts about the inherently subjective nature of mental experience. He writes:

If it be so that the conception of an efficient cause enters into the mind, only from the early conviction we have that we are the efficients of our own voluntary

---

[16] In developing this way of distinguishing between the second and third class of natural signs I have benefited from discussion with Esther Kroeker.

actions, which I think is most probable, the notion of efficiency will be reduced to this, that it is a relation between the cause and the effect, similar to that which is between us and our voluntary actions . . .

Now it is evident, that, to constitute the relation between me and my action, my conception of the action, and will to do it, are essential. For what I never conceived, nor willed, I never did. (*EAP* I. 5, pp. 40/524b–525a)

So far, this passage really amounts to an alternative statement of the stretch of argument summarized in (1.2i)–(1.2v) above: the features that we find in our own experience of ourselves as active—the presence of will and understanding—are extended to all other efficient causes by way of the assumption that we can have no notion of an efficient cause that differs in kind from ourselves. However, Reid draws out the moral of this argument, as follows:

If any man, therefore, affirms, that a being may be the efficient cause of an action, and have power to produce it, which that being can neither conceive nor will, he speaks a language which I do not understand. If he has a meaning, his notion of power and efficiency must be essentially different from mine; and, until he conveys his notion of efficiency to my understanding, I can no more assent to his opinion, than if he should affirm, that a being without life may feel pain. (*EAP* I. 5, p. 40/525a)

The plausibility of the claim that only a living being can feel pain derives from the thought that there is something intrinsically subjective about pain; pain requires a first-personal point of view.[17] But since Reid gives the claim that activity requires a will the very same status as the claim that pain requires life, it seems quite likely that he thinks of the connection between activity and the will as rooted in the thought that there is something inconceivable about exertion unfelt.

Premise (1.3): S Has a Will Only if S Has an Understanding

Premise (1.3) is necessary to establish that causes have minds like ours. If a creature could have a will without having an understanding—if it could aim at the production of events without having the capacity to think about them—then, even given premises (1.1) and (1.2), causes could be entities

---

[17] Another possible motivation: we might think that there would be no point in investing creatures incapable of moving themselves with pain; we might think, that is, that there is no point in giving pain to a thing that can't respond to pain. (Thanks to Paul Hoffman for pointing this out.) In the end, however, I'm not sure that this motivation is much different from that discussed in the main text. After all, what makes a creature capable of responding to pain is its capacity to direct itself in accordance with the states of itself that are accessible solely from a subjective, first-personal perspective.

quite unlike us; they could, that is, be entities endowed with the likes of dormitive virtues or substantial forms. We might imagine such a creature to be striving towards an end without thinking about that end. However, Reid holds that a creature can't will without a conception of what he wills (*EAP* II. 1, p. 60/531*a*; II. 3, p. 76/537*a*). Since conception is an act of the understanding, it follows that possession of a will requires certain basic capacities for thought.

The claim that one cannot will without conceiving of what one wills is somewhat more puzzling than it might, at first, appear. The claim could be interpreted in one of three different ways: as logically necessary, as nomically necessary, or as a principle of rationality. Reid could be asserting that it is a logical impossibility for an agent to will to A without having a conception of A. That is, he might be claiming that the sentence "S willed to A but didn't think about A" implies a contradiction. Alternatively, he might be claiming that it is psychologically impossible to will to A without the requisite conception. That is, he might be claiming that there is an exceptionless law of human psychology that states that all acts of will are accompanied by the conception of that which is willed. Or, he could be making a claim about the cognitive conditions on rational willing. That is, he could be claiming that an agent who wills to A without the appropriate conception is irrational.

The third of these interpretations, under which the claim is a principle of rationality, is ruled out by the following passage:

A man may desire to make a visit to the moon, or to the planet Jupiter, but he cannot will or determine to do it; because he knows it is not in his power. If an insane person should make an attempt, his insanity must first make him believe it to be in his power. (*EAP* II. 1, p. 62/532*b*; see also *EAP* I. 2, p. 19/517*b*)

If the insane, who are irrational, would have to come to believe themselves to be capable of visiting Jupiter in order to will to do it, then irrationality doesn't free one from believing what one wills to be in one's power. However, the belief that an action is in one's power requires a conception of the act, and so creatures with wills are under more than rational pressure to have a conception of what they will.

We can get a hint as to whether Reid accords his claim about the relationship between willing and conception the status of logical or nomic necessity by looking at the way he supports the claim:

Every act of will must have an object. He that wills must will something; and that which he wills is called the object of his volition. As a man cannot think without thinking of something, nor remember without remembering something, so neither can he will without willing something. Every act of will, therefore, must have an object; and the person who wills must have some conception, more or less distinct, of what he wills. (*EAP* II. 1, p. 59/531*b*)

Reid seems to think that the claim that willing requires conception is supported by the fact that thinking and remembering require objects. Reid presents that claim as one of his "principles taken for granted" early in the *Essays on the Intellectual Powers*:

I take it for granted, that in most operations of the mind, there must be an *object* distinct from the operation itself. I cannot see, without seeing something. To see, without having any object of sight, is absurd. I cannot remember, without remembering something... The operations of our minds are denoted, in all languages, by active transitive verbs, which, from their construction in grammar, require not only a person or agent, but likewise an object of the operation. (*EIP* I. 2, p. 44)

The evidence that Reid provides for the claim that seeing and remembering require objects is linguistic: those mental operations are referred to with transitive verbs "in all languages". Further, Reid tells us what status he accords to true claims concerning universal grammatical structures. Such truths are among the "first principles of necessary truths":

There are some first principles that may be called grammatical; such as, that every adjective in a sentence must belong to some substantive expressed or understood; that every complete sentence must have a verb.

Those who have attended to the structure of language, and formed distinct notions of the nature and use of the various parts of speech, perceive, without reasoning, that these, and many other such principles, are necessarily true. (*EIP* VI. 6, p. 491)

Presumably, then, Reid thinks it a necessary truth that transitive verbs take an object, and so thinks it a necessary truth that "thinking", "seeing", "remembering", and "willing" take objects. He must also hold that if a mental act takes an object, then the person engaging in that mental act, *ipso facto*, conceives of the object; to conceive of something just is to engage in a mental act that takes that thing as its object. It is a short step from here to the conclusion that the claim that willing requires conception is a necessary truth.

One might take this to imply that Reid thinks it not merely false to say that a person does not know what he is aiming to do, but logically impossible. If what you are aiming to do is identified with what you are willing to do, and if it is simply logically impossible to will to do something without having a conception of it, then it is logically impossible to be in the dark about one's own aims. However, Reid is much more sensitive to the various ways in which our aims are concealed from us than his claim would seem to imply. For instance, in distinguishing between a genuine virtue, on the one hand, and a mere affective propensity to do the right thing, on the other, he writes:

In practice, indeed, we cannot distinguish them in other men, and with difficulty in ourselves; but in theory, nothing is more easy. The virtue of benevolence is a fixed purpose or resolution to do good when we have opportunity, from a conviction that it is right, and is our duty. The affection of benevolence is a propensity to do good, from natural constitution or habit, without regard to rectitude or duty. (*EAP* II. 3, p. 86/540*b*)[18]

Although there are other differences alluded to here between the genuinely benevolent and those who act out of benevolent affection, Reid thinks that they differ in the reasons for which they act: the genuinely benevolent, and not those with benevolent affection, act out of the conviction that their acts are right and dutiful. Further, we have trouble determining, in our own case, whether we are acting out of benevolence or out of benevolent affection. It seems to follow that we have trouble determining what our aims are in acting. In choosing the act, am I choosing because of its "rectitude"? Or am I choosing it merely because through it I can get something that I want? These questions would appear to have meaning for Reid, and yet if conception of what one wills is entailed by willing, they would seem to have no meaning at all. To have doubt about what one wills, on that view, would not be to will at all.[19]

[18] This passage is discussed at some length in Ch. 4.

[19] Terence Cuneo has suggested to me in correspondence that the problem raised here is more easily solved, even, than I take it to be. Cuneo suggests that if an agent has a conception of his action as, say, a benevolent act, then he has a conception of his action, even if the act is not, in fact, a benevolent act, but performed, instead, from benevolent affection. The appeal of Cuneo's solution to the problem comes from thinking that one can conceive of an act (or an object for that matter) under a false description and thus be mistaken about the act's features while successfully conceiving of the act. While a full defense would take us too far afield, I hold, instead, that there is no such thing for Reid as conceiving of an act *under a description*. To conceive of an object as, say, hard is to have a thought about a property, hardness, and to have a thought about the object, and to further judge that the property belongs to the object. However, the very same analysis of what it is to conceive of an act as possessing a particular property (benevolence, say) cannot be employed because acts are individuated, in part, by the motives for the sake of which they are performed. To conceive of a benevolent act as performed for something other than a benevolent motive is not to conceive of the benevolent act at all.

In fact, however, Reid's doubts about our capacity to determine when we are acting from benevolence and when from benevolent affection are consistent with his claim that to will is, necessarily, to conceive of what one wills. Reid denies that those who act from benevolent affection do, indeed, choose to act. They act, instead, from "natural constitution or habit" (*EAP* II. 3, p. 86/540*b*). And, Reid explicitly distinguishes those who act from natural constitution or habit from those who act from choice on the grounds that the latter, and not the former, have a conception of the act at which they aim:

> By [appeal to the motivating state's having an object], things done voluntarily are distinguished from things done merely from instinct, or merely from habit.
>
> A healthy child, some hours after its birth, feels the sensation of hunger, and, if applied to the breast, sucks and swallows its food very perfectly. We have no reason to think, that, before it ever sucked, it has any conception of that complex operation, or how it is performed. It cannot, therefore, with propriety, be said, that it wills to suck. (*EAP* II. 1, p. 59/531*b*)

In fact, Reid goes on to say that the ends at which those who act from instinct aim are not their own: "[Animals] act by some inward blind impulse, of which the efficient cause is hid from us; and though there is an end evidently intended by the action, this intention is not in the animal, but in its Maker" (*EAP* II. 1, p. 60/531*b*).[20] So, it seems to follow, our difficulty in determining whether we act from genuine benevolence or merely from benevolent affection is a difficulty in determining whether we actually choose to act or, instead, act from instinct or habit instilled in us to serve the ends of some other efficient cause.

But if we can be uncertain as to whether our motivating mental state is, or is not, a choice, then in what sense do our choices wear their activity on their face? This question seems particularly pressing in the present context when we recall that an important part of Reid's justification for the claim that the power to do something requires the power to exert that power—that is, premise (1.1)—is that exertions of power are, necessarily, expressions of the power to act; they are, necessarily, actions. But if we can be in doubt as to whether the ends at which we aim are our own, then it seems that we can be in doubt as to whether we are aiming or merely being aimed; we can be in doubt about the degree to which the mental state that moves us is, indeed, an action.

---

[20] Reid does not think that every time an animal acts it does so from a "blind impulse", because he doesn't think that every time an animal acts it acts from instinct; sometimes animals act with intent (cf. *EAP* III. 2. i, p. 118/551*b*). This is consistent, however, with the view that no creature that acts from instinct chooses to act as it does.

However, another strand in Reid's conception of the will may provide him with a way of responding to this problem. Reid consistently distinguishes between those things of which we are conscious and those to which we attend and claims "that we are conscious of many things to which we give little or no attention" (*EIP* I. 2. p. 42). Further, Reid claims that every volition is "accompanied with an effort to execute that which we willed" (*EAP* II. 1, p. 63/532b) and after having noted that sometimes the effort is so small that we don't notice it, he writes: "This effort we are conscious of, if we will but give attention to it; and there is nothing in which we are in a more strict sense active" (*EAP* II. 1, p. 63/533a). This remark seems to suggest that what we are really conscious of when we choose, and which qualifies our choice as an act, is the feeling of effort involved in every volition. But since these efforts can be difficult to attend to, it can be difficult to tell if one is, in fact, exercising one's power or, instead, acting from instinct.

The will's object—that which we choose—is necessarily something about which we think, and so we are, in a sense, always aware of that at which we aim. However, since we may fail to attend to objects of consciousness, we can fail to attend to that which we consciously will. What this implies is that Reid lies on a cusp between the view that the mind is entirely transparent to itself, and the view that our motives are often entirely hidden from our conscious view. The fact that what moves one is an object of consciousness is not enough for it to be something apprehended by the mind; it must also be an object of attention.[21] But, still, the idea of a mental state the object of which is entirely hidden from view is a contradiction; such a mental state has no object at all. It is this latter view that supports premise (1.3), and, in turn, Reid's argument for the claim that efficient causes have will and understanding.

Conclusion

Reid's argument from the power to exert coheres tightly with a trio of very natural things to believe: that we are, necessarily, active with respect to our

---

[21] Also relevant: "A man may, no doubt, know with certainty the principles from which he himself acts, because he is conscious of them. But this knowledge requires an attentive reflection upon the operations of his own mind, which is very rarely found. It is perhaps more easy to find a man who has formed a just notion of the character of man in general, or of those of his familiar acquaintance, than one who has a just notion of his own character" (*EAP* III. 1. i, p. 97/544a–b).

choices; that we are incapable of conceiving of mental powers possessing subjective, qualitative features different in kind from our own; and that in willing we think about what we will. If all three of these things are true, then in ascribing powers to objects lacking in minds we are implicitly animating the inanimate. To think of the sun as something with the power to burn our skins, or of the tornado as a being with the power to wreak havoc, whether we know it or not, is to adopt the point of view of those objects and to think of them as willing the burns or the chaos. The position that is shown, by Reid's argument, to be unstable, then, is that of the philosopher who believes active power to be ubiquitous, found, even, in ordinary mindless objects; if such objects had powers, they would also be capable of directing those powers towards particular ends and would therefore be capable of willing, something that nothing without a mind can do. Of course, to show that active power presupposes will and understanding is not to show that there are any beings endowed with active power, much less that human beings are among them. Reid's reasons for believing these claims will be taken up in Chapters 3 and 4.

2

From Power to Mind: An Argument from the Power to Do Otherwise

Although it is not developed in anything like the detail that Reid develops the argument from the power to exert, Reid does offer another argument for the claim that efficient causes must have will and understanding. He writes: "Power to produce any effect implies power not to produce it. We can conceive no way in which power may be determined to one of these rather than the other, in a being that has no will" (*EAP* I. 5, p. 35/523*a*). Reid doesn't explicitly say that this is a different argument from the argument discussed in Chapter 1, but it is hard to see how it could be construed to be either a restatement of that argument, or a statement of an argument in favor of one of the first argument's premises. Reid seems to be expressing a very different idea. His idea here seems to be that the power to elect one course of conduct over another—to elect one route *rather than* another—requires a will. This would not, all by itself, show that anything endowed with active power has a will, for it would remain possible that a thing with active power was only capable of doing one thing, so never had to elect one course of conduct over another, and so didn't require a will. However, that possibility is precluded by the fact that the power to do something entails possession of the power not to do it. We could formalize this line of thought like this:

(2.1) If S has the power to A, then S has the power not to A.

(2.2) If S has the power to A and the power not to A, then S has the power to A-rather-than-not A.[1]

---

[1] Notice that premise (2.2) is not explicitly mentioned by Reid. However, his argument requires it. Still, the fact that he never mentions it explicitly is itself in need of explanation, and an explanation for that fact will be provided shortly.

(2.3) If S has the power to A-rather-than-not A, then S has a will.
∴ If S has a power, then S has a will.

If we add premise (1.3) from the argument from the power to exert—the premise linking will with understanding—we reach the conclusion that wherever there is power there is will and understanding. As was the case with the argument from the power to exert, each of the premises in the argument from the power to do otherwise requires discussion.

Premise (2.1): If S Has the Power to A, then S Has the Power Not to A

Premise (2.1) is the most natural way of characterizing what Reid means when he says "Power to produce any effect implies power not to produce it." If we assume that the power not to A is the same thing as the power to prevent A from occurring, then (2.1) glosses Reid's remark as the claim that anything that one is capable of bringing about is also something one is capable of preventing from occurring. So understood, however, (2.1) seems to be amenable to counterexamples of which Reid was surely aware.[2] Locke, for instance, offers the following famous example:

[S]uppose a Man be carried, whilst fast asleep, into a Room, where is a Person he longs to see and speak with; and be there locked fast in, beyond his Power to get out: he awakes, and is glad to find himself in so desirable Company, which he stays willingly in, *i.e.* preferrs his stay to going away. I ask, Is not this stay voluntary? I think, no Body will doubt it: and yet being locked fast in, 'tis evident he is not at liberty not to stay, he has not freedom to be gone. (*Essay Concerning Human Understanding*, II. XXI. 10)[3]

Since the staying of the man in the locked room is one of the man's actions, it follows that it is an exercise of the man's active power to stay in the room.[4] But the man seems to lack the power not to stay in the room. If this

---

[2] While he was almost surely aware of such examples, there is nowhere that I know of in which Reid explicitly discusses them.

[3] For discussion, cf. E. J. Lowe, "Necessity and the Will in Locke's Theory of Action", *History of Philosophy Quarterly*, 3/2 (1986), 149–63; Gideon Yaffe, "Locke on Suspending, Refraining and the Freedom to Will", *History of Philosophy Quarterly*, 18/4 (2001), 373–92.

[4] One might wonder if Locke would agree with this claim. Perhaps Locke's notion of the voluntary, we might say, allows for events to be voluntary even if they are not actions. This line of thought is encouraged by the fact that Locke seems to be implying that an event is voluntary just in case it accords with a person's preferences. This line of Locke interpretation, however, overlooks the fact that Locke uses the term "prefer" interchangeably with the term "volition" and defines volition to be "an Act of the Mind knowingly exerting that Dominion it takes it self to have over any part of the Man" (*Essay Concerning Human Understanding*, II. XXI. 25; see also II. XXI. 72). For discussion, see Gideon Yaffe, *Liberty Worth the Name*, ch. 2, esp. pp. 88–98.

is the correct analysis of the example, then (2.1) is false. The challenge that such examples pose to (2.1) is so formidable that there is a strong temptation to deny that Reid actually meant (2.1) when he said that "Power to produce any effect implies power not to produce it."[5] However, as will be argued here, Reid can defend (2.1) even in the face of examples like Locke's.

The temptation, in response to such examples, is to distinguish what the agent has the power to do (namely, stay in the room voluntarily) from what he lacks the power to avoid (namely, stay in the room). After all, we might say, the man in the locked room has the power not to stay in the room *voluntarily*: to do so, all he needs to do is not exercise his power to stay in the room. If he tries to leave, for instance, he exerts a power to do something other than stay in the room voluntarily, and hence he has the power not to stay in the room voluntarily. The lock on the door, we might say, that is, limits where the man can be, not what accounts for his being there; he retains the ability to stay under his own power, or stay only because he doesn't have the power not to.[6]

This move is somewhat less natural when used to respond to another example of Locke's, an example that Locke himself takes to illustrate the very same point illustrated by the example of the man in the locked room:

> [A] Palsie or the Stocks hinder [a man's] Legs from obeying the determination of his Mind, if it would thereby transferr his Body to another Place. In all [such cases] there is want of *Freedom*, though the sitting still even of a Paralytick, whilst he preferrs it to a removal, is truly voluntary. (*Essay Concerning Human Understanding,* II. XXI. 11)

The paralytic seems to have the power to stay where he is, but no power to move. If so, then (2.1) is false. Although it might be correct to say that the paralytic still has both the power to sit still *voluntarily* and the power not to sit still *voluntarily*, it is strained to say this because the paralytic engages in precisely the same bodily movements whether he sits still voluntarily or not. In contrast, if the man in the locked room stays involuntarily, then he paces about, or struggles with the door; he engages in movements that are

---

[5] In fact, William Rowe holds that, ultimately, Reid did not intend (2.1) but rather the following weaker claim. If S has the power to cause A, then S has the power not to cause A. Since the power not to cause A is consistent with the inability to prevent A—perhaps one cannot prevent A from being caused by someone else—Rowe's principle is weaker than (2.1). See William Rowe, *Thomas Reid on Freedom and Morality* (Ithaca, NY: Cornell University Press, 1991), esp. pp. 49, 85.

[6] There is a substantial amount of literature on this "flicker of freedom" approach to examples of the overdetermination of action. For a start, see John Fischer, *The Metaphysics of Free Will: An Essay on Control* (Oxford, Blackwell Press, 1994), esp. pp. 134–47.

different from those of a person content to stay. But, if we wish to continue to defend the view that the man in the locked room does have the two-way power to stay or not stay *voluntarily*, we might say that what matters is not that the agent would visibly be involved in a different activity were he not to exert his power to stay, or his power to sit still. What matters, rather, is that there is something that he can do or not do. In the case of the man in the locked room, he can engage, or not engage, in certain bodily movements that are unhindered by the lock on the door, and he can do so because he can engage, or not engage, in a certain mental act, namely, the act of exerting his power to stay in the room. In the case of the paralytic, he can engage, or not engage, only in the mental act, the act of exerting his power to sit still. His power to exert or not to exert his power to sit still is not affected by the source of his paralysis.

It seems, then, that the claim that agents in examples like Locke's always do have some two-way power—there is always something that they have both the power to bring about and the power to prevent from occurring—rests on the claim that agents always have both the power to exert their powers to act and the power to prevent the occurrence of exertions of power. To rely on this claim in order to respond to apparent counterexamples to (2.1), however, is simply to apply premise (2.1) to a particular power: it is simply to insist, without argument, that the power to exert is always accompanied by the power to prevent that exertion. Thus, the proposed analysis of examples like Locke's, under which the man in the locked room who cannot but stay is attributed with both a power to stay *voluntarily* and a power to prevent a *voluntary* stay, simply begs the question.[7]

Notice, however, that even if we admit that in cases such as Locke's the agent always has some power to act that is accompanied by the power not to act, we have not thereby vindicated (2.1) in the face of the examples. After all, (2.1) claims that *every* power to act is conjoined with the power not to act. Locke's examples invalidate this claim even if there is always *some* power to be found that is accompanied by the appropriate power to act otherwise. Even if the man in the locked room has the power to stay

---

[7] Notice that this is also true of the claim that Rowe attributes to Reid, mentioned in n. 5. After all, the power to avoid being the cause of an event reduces to the power to prevent the occurrence of an exertion of power. Hence, the claim that Rowe attributes to Reid amounts to this: if S has the power to exert his power, then he has the power to prevent that exertion from occurring. This is just a special case of (2.1) and so requires defense along lines very similar to those needed to defend (2.1). Unless exertion of power is very different from any other kind of action, (2.1) will be just as defensible, or indefensible, as Rowe's principle.

voluntarily, and the power not to stay voluntarily, he still has the power to stay and lacks the power not to stay; he can stay if he likes, but he simply can't leave. There is at least one power to act that the man possesses despite lacking the power not to so act, and one is enough to show (2.1) to be false. Or, at least, so it seems.

If Reid holds (2.1), he must face Locke's examples, then, and he cannot simply dismiss them through employing the strategy just discussed. He cannot, that is, simply search for something that the agent both has the power to produce and to prevent. There are two ways to defend (2.1) in the face of such examples: Reid could either assert that the man in the locked room has the power *not* to stay in the room, or he could deny that the man in the locked room has the power *to* stay in the room. The prospect for success of the former of these two options seems dim, and Reid would agree. Consider, for instance, the following passage:

[A] being may have a power at one time which it has not at another. It may commonly have a power, which, at a particular time, it has not. Thus, a man may commonly have power to walk or to run; but he has not this power when asleep, or when he is confined by superior force. In common language, he may be said to have a power which he cannot then exert. But this popular expression means only that he commonly has this power, and will have it when the cause is removed which at present deprives him of it. (*EAP* IV. 2, p. 269/603*b*)

It is important to Reid that the man in the locked room should lack the power not to stay, since it is important to Reid that if an agent has the power to act in a particular way, then all that needs to occur for him to act that way is that he should exert that power; to leave, the man in the locked room, by contrast, would first need to acquire a key. Thus, Reid would deny that the man in the locked room has the power not to stay, since no matter how hard the man tries, he is going to stay in the room. The only sense in which it is right to say that the man in the locked room has the power not to stay is the sense identified in the passage just quoted: were the lock on the door removed, then he would have that power, which he presently lacks.

So, it seems that, if Reid is to defend (2.1), he must deny that the man in the locked room has the power to stay in the room. This option, too, encounters obstacles. If Reid is to take this route, must he deny that the man stays in the room voluntarily (the very point that Locke, anyway, took to be beyond question)? Voluntary action is the paradigm case of a state of the agent, or an event in which he engages, with respect to which the agent is active. Reid notes that the term "action" can be used broadly to mean any bit of behavior that is voluntary, involuntary, or "mixed", or narrowly to mean only voluntary behavior, or behavior springing from an exercise of the will (cf. *EAP* III. 1. i, p. 94/543a). Thus, every case of genuine action—where "action" is used in the narrow sense—is a voluntary action. It might appear to follow, also, that an agent's behavior can be voluntary only if he has the active power to so act. If so, then, if Reid is to deny that the man has the power to stay, he must deny that the man stays voluntarily. However, if the man's staying springs from an act of will on his part, then the man does stay voluntarily; if you engage in a bit of behavior, and your behavior is appropriately related to an act of will on your part in favor of it, then the behavior is voluntary. Thus, it appears that Reid must also deny that the man *chooses* to stay. Although the man does direct himself to stay and stays as a result of the direction he gives himself, if the possession of active power is a necessary condition of voluntary action, then Reid must deny that the mental state of directing himself in this manner is, in fact, a volition.

But what possible reason could Reid have for believing that the man in the locked room does not choose to stay in the room? All of the features ordinarily thought of as distinctive of volition are present in the case: the man stays for a reason—he finds "desirable Company" in the room; he has a conception of the act at which he directs himself; there is no reason to think him unconscious of the mental state through which he directs himself to stay; or of the reasons on the basis of which he so directs himself; nor is there any reason to think that he lacks the belief that staying is within his power—for all Locke says, the man may not even know that the door is locked, and so even if (2.1) is true and he believes it to be true, he may have no good reason to believe himself to lack the power to stay.

Reid can offer a better defense of (2.1) by agreeing that all genuine action—all of an agent's behavior springing from the exercise of active power—is voluntary action, while denying that all voluntary behavior is genuine action. Then, he might say, the man in the locked room stays voluntarily, but lacks the power to stay, for his voluntary behavior in this case is not genuine action. If this position can be maintained, (2.1) will be shown to be consistent with Locke's examples, since the man in the locked room will lack *both* the power to act and the power not to act, despite the fact that he acts voluntarily, and so he will not serve as an example of someone possessed with a power to produce a certain result, but lacking a power to prevent its occurrence. This approach, however, raises a question: what, if anything, helps to make plausible the claim that an agent can engage in voluntary behavior while lacking the power to act?

Given that Reid thinks of exertions of power as identical to volitions, it might seem that an agent cannot make a choice unless he has the power to act as he chooses. This would be a counterintuitive position—it seems that people choose to do all sorts of things they can't do—and Reid does not hold it: he writes, for instance, of a man who loses his voice in the night, and chooses to speak in the morning before discovering that he's lost his voice (*EAP* II. 1, p. *62/532b*). Reid does deny that an agent can choose to do something that he can't do if he believes that he can't do it—belief that one has the power to do something is a necessary condition of choosing to do it, he thinks (*EAP* II. 1, p. *62/532b*)—but since that belief can be false, this does not preclude the possibility that the agent chooses to do something he can't do.[8] In standard cases of choice without power the agent does not, in fact, do what he chooses to do. The evidence that such agents lack the power to do as they choose is that they fail to do it despite their best efforts. If the analysis of Locke's example under consideration at this point is correct, then that is an example quite unlike the standard examples, for Locke's man chooses to stay and does precisely what he chooses to do. What grounds are there for denying that he has the power to do as he does?

The best answer seems to be that the man would do what he does— stay—no matter what. It is true that he will not stay voluntarily no matter what—if he doesn't choose to stay, he'll stay involuntarily. But as pointed out already, that doesn't help Reid to defend (2.1) since (2.1) makes a general claim about all powers, namely, that each is accompanied by the power to prevent what one has the power to cause. Notice that if Reid holds the following principle, then there is good reason to think that the man in the locked room does not have the power to stay:

Efficient-Causal Exclusivity: Every event that has an efficient cause has one, and only one, efficient cause.

---

[8] So, when Reid writes, "[T]here can be no exertion without power" (*EAP* I. 1, p. 9/514*a*) he cannot mean that to exert oneself one must have the power to do as one tries. There are two other possible interpretations of this remark. Reid might mean that there can be no exertion *without the belief* that one has the power to do as one exerts oneself to do. Alternatively, he might mean that no event can occur—including an exertion—unless some being has the power to bring about that very event. This would be to say that one cannot exert oneself to act unless one has the power to exert oneself to act; this would leave open the possibility that one exerts oneself while lacking the power to act as one is trying to act.

Given that there is a law linking the presence of a person in a locked room at a particular time to the person's remaining in the room at a later time (*ceteris paribus*)—that is, the man's staying is physically caused by conditions that do not include the man's exertion of power—and given that (Reid thinks) behind all physical causal interactions is an efficient cause who authored the relevant law, it follows that there is some agent other than the man in the room who is an efficient cause of the man's staying.[9] If Reid holds the principle of Efficient-Causal Exclusivity, then there is a case to be made that that agent, and not the man in the room, is the cause of the man's staying. However, since the man did indeed make an effort to stay in the room, and since if he had the power to stay, the fact of his power together with his exertion would have qualified him as the efficient cause of his staying, it follows that he lacks the power to stay; given that he exerted himself, if he's not the cause, he must not have the power. Given that the man will stay no matter what he does, there is a competitor for the title of efficient cause of his staying; and given the principle of Efficient-Causal Exclusivity, the presence of a competitor as efficient cause of his staying precludes the possibility that he is the cause.

Reid commits himself to the principle of Efficient-Causal Exclusivity in a different, but related context. He writes:

It is possible . . . that what we call the immediate effects of our power, may not be so in the strictest sense. Between the will to produce the effect, and the production of it, there may be agents or instruments of which we are ignorant.

This may leave some doubt, whether we be, in the strictest sense, the efficient cause of the voluntary motions of our own body.   (*EAP* I. 7, pp. 50–1/528b)

It is worth noting that in this passage Reid clearly allows that an action could be voluntary despite the fact that the agent is not the cause of it. But the pressing question that this passage raises is why it should be that, even if there are "agents or instruments" that cause our bodily motions on the occasion of our willing them, we would not count as the causes of those movements. Imagine that there is such an agent—God, say—who causes our bodies to move when we will them to. This would not preclude the possibility that we have the power to move our bodies, exert that power when we will to move them, and thereby count as the efficient cause of our bodily movements. The fact that God participates—causes our

---

[9] What, exactly, is meant by the claim that "behind all physical causal interactions is an efficient cause who authored the relevant law" is discussed in Chs. 3 and 4.

movements—would only suggest that we are not their efficient cause if Reid disallows the possibility that a single event, a single bodily movement in this case, could have more than one efficient cause. Since Reid thinks that we would not be the efficient causes of our bodily movements if there were agents and instruments who efficiently caused them, he must accept the Efficient-Causal Exclusivity principle.[10]

The principle of Efficient-Causal Exclusivity does not tell us how to adjudicate disputes among competitors for the title of cause. When there is an effect and more than one agent that exerted itself to produce it—as is the case in Locke's examples, given that the man will stay even if he doesn't exert himself to stay—the principle of Efficient-Causal Exclusivity tells us that one and only of those agents is the cause. How do we determine which one? We might think that the cause is the agent whose exertion was required for the effect. However, the man in the locked room and the author of the laws governing the relative strengths of locks and men seem to be on a par in this regard. Even if the man had willed to leave, he would have stayed; however, even if the laws were such that the man would have broken the lock had he tried, he still would have stayed.

In general, Reid seems to think that, if an item of behavior is subsumable under a law that links it to an antecedent condition that does not include the agent's exertion of power, then the agent is not the cause of the behavior. He claims, for instance, that if the Principle of Sufficient Reason were granted it would follow that we aren't free: "The determination of the will is an event for which there must be a sufficient reason, that is, something previous, which was necessarily followed by that determination, and could not be followed by any other determination; therefore it was necessary" (*EAP* IV. 9, p. 328/625a). The fact that the agent's act of will was "necessary"—that is, caused by something other than the agent (cf. *EAP* IV. 1, p. 259/599b)—would not follow from the fact that it was subsumable under a law linking it to "something previous" unless it were impossible for both the author of that law and the agent to be the cause of

---

[10] There are other passages that support the same point, and for the same reasons. For instance: "[I do not] know how my volition and effort to move my hand, produces a certain motion in the nerves. I am conscious that in this there is something which I do not comprehend, though I believe He that made me comprehends it perfectly ... I am uncertain whether I be truly and properly the agent in the first motion; for I can suppose, that, whenever I will to move my hand, the Deity, or some other agent, produces the first motion in my body—which was the opinion of Malebranche" (*COR*, app. A, p. 247). Why would Reid think that the Malebranchian hypothesis rules out the possibility that we are the efficient causes of our own bodily motions? He must be accepting the principle of Efficient-Causal Exclusivity.

the exertion; that is, Reid must be assuming the principle of Efficient-Causal Exclusivity. Further, between the competitors for the title of cause of the agent's act of will—the author of the relevant law, on the one hand, and the agent on the other—Reid gives the clear advantage to the author of the law. That agent was the cause of the agent's act of will rather than the agent himself. While it is not clear what justifies this test for adjudicating disputes for title of cause, when the test is applied to the case of the man in the locked room, we reach the result that the author of the laws that insure that the man will stay in the room is the cause of the man's staying, rather than the man himself. It follows, then, that the man lacks the power to stay in the room, and, in turn that the example is no counterexample to (2.1).

The discussion of Locke's examples just offered can be presented as a *reductio ad absurdum* argument for (2.1) as follows:

(2.1i)   For some agent S and event A, S has the power to A, but lacks the power not to A (the negation of (2.1)).

(2.1ii)   A will occur even if S does not exert his power to A.

(2.1iii)   There is some antecedent condition that does not include S's exertion of his power to A which is the physical cause of A.

(2.1iv)   If an event has a physical cause, then the author of the relevant law is an efficient cause of the event.[11]

(2.1v)   A has some efficient cause other than S.

(2.1vi)   If S exerts his power to A, A will occur and will have two efficient causes.

(2.1vii)   For every event there is one and only one efficient cause. (the principle of Efficient-Causal Exclusivity)

∴ (2.1ii) is false; that is, (2.1) is true.

While it would be an exaggeration to suggest that Reid has this argument in mind, the argument makes it possible for Reid to respond to examples from his own time that would invalidate his claim, and draws on claims that he himself depends on in other contexts. The argument, then, provides a Reidian defense of Reid's own premise.

---

[11] This premise amounts to the rule, discussed above, for adjudicating disputes between competitors for the title of "cause". When coupled with the principle of Efficient-Causal Exclusivity, (2.1iv) says that the winner in such a dispute is the author of the law under which the event can be subsumed.

Premise (2.2): If S Has the Power to A and the Power Not to A, then S Has the Power to A-rather-than-Not A

To appreciate the content of (2.2), notice that the power to do one-thing-rather-than-another is not the same as the power to do that thing in conditions in which it is impossible to do both it and the other. The reason is that, while an action correctly describable as "A-ing-rather-than-B-ing" is a species of a genus of action describable as "A-ing", there are other members of the genus that do not fall under the species, and this is true regardless of whether or not the conditions preclude the possibility of performing both A and B. So, for instance, imagine that I don't have enough eggs to make both an omelet and a souffle, although I have enough to make one or the other; and imagine that I make an omelet. It doesn't follow that I make an-omelet-rather-than-a-souffle. If, for instance, I don't have any idea how many eggs are required to make a souffle—I might not even know that souffles require eggs to make—then it might not be right to say that I'm making an-omelet-rather-than-a-souffle. Of course, if I consider whether or not to make a souffle, I realize that I can't make both it and an omelet, and I decide to make an omelet instead, then I make an-omelet-rather-than-a-souffle. In this case, my action fits both the description "making an omelet" and the description "making an omelet rather than a souffle", while in the first case my action falls under only the first of these two descriptions.[12]

The point can be extended to powers. A person could lack the power to make an-omelet-rather-than-a-souffle while possessing the power to make an omelet. Such is the case in the example of the person who knows nothing of souffle-making and doesn't realize that his making an omelet will preclude him from making a souffle (assuming he lacks the power to gain the relevant knowledge); still, he has the power to make an omelet. Since every

---

[12] The point made here serves as an objection to a point made by Timothy O'Connor in a different context. O'Connor responds to the following objection to agent causalism: the agent-causalist is committed to the claim that there is no explanation for why the events that the agent causes occurred *rather than* other incompatible events; after all, the agent-causalist cannot say that the agent would do something differently in order to cause something other than what he actually caused, because then the agent-causalist slips into an event-causal conception of the agent's role. O'Connor responds that there is no difference between an event occurring and that event occurring rather than another. (See Timothy O'Connor, *Persons and Causes: The Metaphysics of Free Will* (New York: Oxford University Press, 2000) cf. pp. 75–6.) However, if the point made in the main text is correct, then O'Connor is mistaken; there is a difference between performing an action and performing that act rather than something else. Since actions are a species of event, O'Connor's claim is false.

time a person makes an-omelet-rather-than-a-souffle, he also makes an omelet, it follows that anyone who has the power to make an-omelet-rather-than-a-souffle also has the power to make an omelet. (2.2), however, makes a claim that does not follow immediately from the points just made. (2.2) is an instance of a more general principle that turns out to be false:

> (2.2*a*) If S has the power to A and the power to B, and it is not possible to both A and B, then S has the power to A-rather-than-B.

According to (2.2*a*), to continue the example, a person cannot have the power to make an omelet and yet lack the power to make an-omelet-rather-than-a-souffle if he has the power to make a souffle. According to (2.2*a*), possession of both the power to make an omelet and the power to make a souffle amounts to possession of the power to make an-omelet-rather-than-a-souffle and a-souffle-rather-than-an-omelet (in conditions under which one can't do both).

If (2.2*a*) is true, then so is (2.2). Unfortunately, (2.2*a*) admits of counterexamples. For instance, say that I have the power to make an omelet and the power to make a souffle, and I would like to make both, and I think, falsely, that I have enough eggs to make both. My false belief would seem to prevent me from making an-omelet-rather-than-a-souffle. If I'd like to make both, I can't conceive of my action as that of precluding performance of the other act unless I know that I cannot do both; and unless I can conceive of my act that way, I can't make an-omelet-rather-than-a-souffle.

If Reid were to accept (2.2) on the basis of (2.2*a*), then his argument would fail. (2.2), however, is (2.2*a*) restricted to the case where B is the act of preventing the occurrence of A. This is not the case in our counterexample to (2.2*a*); to make a souffle is not necessarily to prevent the making of an omelet. This encourages the thought that (2.2) might be true, even though (2.2*a*) is false. After all, it seems unlikely that a person could have the power to prevent A from occurring and not know that, by exercising that power, A would be prevented from occurring. The action of the agent who lacked that knowledge would not be intentional under the description "preventing A from occurring", and so he could not be said to have the active power to prevent A from occurring. To determine whether or not (2.2) is true, we need to imagine a slightly different example, one in which the alternative act is the act of preventing the primary act. For instance, imagine, instead, that I have the power to make an omelet (plenty of eggs, training at the best cooking schools, etc.) and the power to prevent an omelet from being made (I can throw those eggs out the window, for instance). In that case, do I also have the power to make an-omelet-rather-than-preventing-an-omelet-from-being-made? That is, do I also have the power to make an omelet and thereby intentionally preclude myself from preventing an omelet from being made? If the answer is "yes", then (2.2) is true.

We cannot say that the answer to this question is "yes" on the grounds that every time I exercise my power to make an omelet, when I have the power to prevent an omelet from being made, I thereby perform an action that is intentional under the description "making an omelet rather than preventing one from being made". After all, I might give no thought whatsoever to the fact that by making the omelet I thereby preclude the possibility that such an occurrence will be prevented. I needn't conceive of myself, for instance, as a crusader against those who want to prevent the making of omelets. I might just be hungry. Even given that I have the power to do the-one-thing-rather-than-the-other, I might simply exercise my power to do the one, simpliciter.

Still, there is a compelling reason to think that the power to A, and the power not to, entail the power to A-rather-than-not: *given that the agent has the power to A, anything that would prevent the agent from A-ing-rather-than-not would also prevent the agent from preventing A.* In other words, to lack the power to A-rather-than-not is to lack the power to prevent A from occurring. To see this, note first that the conditions that eliminate an agent's power to A-rather-than-not are of two sorts: there are those that take away the agent's power to A simpliciter, and there are those that do not do so, but still take away the power to A-rather-than-not. Conditions of the first sort are not relevant to our purposes since it is assumed that the agent has the power to A simpliciter. So, the question is what sorts of conditions eliminate the power to A-rather-than-not without eliminating the power to A simpliciter? Since the only difference between A-ing-rather-than-not and A-ing simpliciter derives from the motive that the agent has for A-ing, and the agent's corresponding conception of the action, it follows that the only relevant conditions that eliminate the power to A-rather-than-not are those that make it impossible for the agent to conceive of the act of A-ing as the act of closing the door to not A-ing. That is, what makes an act of A-ing an instance of A-ing-rather-than-not is just that the agent thinks of his act in a certain way; he thinks of it as the act of making sure that an A is not prevented from occurring, something that he might have motives to do quite independent of those that he has for A-ing simpliciter. But an agent who lacks the capacity to conceive of an act as the prevention of the prevention of A must also lack the capacity to conceive of an act as the prevention of A. Such an agent, however, cannot have the power to prevent A, since that power requires that the agent conceive of his act as the prevention of A, and thus that the agent have the capacity to so conceive of his act.

It is worth illustrating this rather abstract point with an example. Imagine that I have the power to sign a petition and the power to prevent my signature from appearing on the petition. Imagine further that I'm a member of a group that has traditionally been excluded from signing petitions. I might sign the petition because I believe in the cause the petition is meant to support, or I might sign the petition because I want to see to it that my name is not prevented from appearing on the petition. If I sign the petition for the second of these two reasons, then I sign-rather-than-not; part of my reason for signing is to see to it that my signature is not prevented from appearing. If I sign for the first reason, then I sign simpliciter. Now imagine that some condition prevents me from signing-rather-than-not without preventing me from signing. How does the condition do this? It must prevent me from conceiving of my act as insuring that my signature will appear on the petition. Perhaps, for instance, I'm mentally handicapped and simply incapable of hypothetical thinking; I can't think about what I didn't do and will not do, but only about what I did do and will do. However, in such a case my mental condition will also eliminate my power to prevent my signature from appearing on the petition. To have that power, I have to conceive of something that I don't do—sign the petition—and act in such a way as to prevent that from occurring. This example illustrates the general point that an agent who lacks the power to act-rather-than-not must also lack the power not to act. If this general point is correct, then so is (2.2).

The argument for premise (2.2) just offered can be put more formally like so:

(2.2i) S has the power not to A only if S has the power to A-rather-than-not.

(2.2ii) S has the power to A only if S has the power not to A. (Premise (2.1))

(2.2iii) S has the power to A only if S has the power to A-rather-than-not.

∴ (S has the power to A and the power not to A) only if (S has the power to A-rather-than-not). (Premise (2.2))

As was mentioned above (in n. 1) Reid makes no explicit mention of premise (2.2), although the argument from the power to do otherwise requires the premise. We are now in a position to see why Reid does not mention (2.2) explicitly: (2.2) is really just an instance of (2.1). To see this, we need only reflect for a moment on the phrase "the power not to A" which has been used synonomously with "the power to prevent A from occurring". Used in this way, (2.1) implies that the power not to A entails the power not to prevent A. Given how the phrase "the power not to act" is being used, the power not to prevent A is just the power to prevent A from being prevented. That power is identical to the power to A-rather-than-not; it is the power to A in order to see to it that nothing prevents A from occurring; this is the power exercised by the man in our example who signs the petition in order to see to it that he is not prevented from signing. (2.2i), then, is really a tautology. Since the only other premise in the argument for (2.2) is (2.1), once (2.1) is stated there is no more need to state premise (2.2) than there is to state a tautology.

Premise (2.3): If S Has the Power to A-rather-than-Not A, then S Has a Will

In reconstructing Reid's reason for believing (2.3), it is worth drawing further attention to a point made in discussion of premise (2.2): there may be no intrinsic difference between the act of the person who acts simpliciter and the act of the person who acts that-way-rather-than-not. An agent who makes an-omelet-rather-than-a-souffle might engage in precisely the same bodily movements as the agent who makes the omelet simpliciter. What this implies is that the difference between the two acts must be determined by something other than the intrinsic properties of the bodily movements in question. Further, it seems clear that the difference is to be found in the conception that the two agents have of their respective acts, and the role that that conception plays in motivating the act in question: the agent who As-rather-than-not has a conception of his act that includes the act of not doing A—he thinks of his A-ing as being the act of preventing something else—while the agent who As simpliciter may have a conception of the act without any conception whatsoever of what will not happen due to his action. The agent who As-rather-than-not sees the value of A-ing as consisting, in part, in the fact that by doing so he insures that an A-ing will not be prevented; the value of what he does, he thinks, derives in part from the comparison between what he does and what he, thereby, does not do. The agent who As simpliciter might see the value of his A-ing to derive solely from what happens, and not from what doesn't happen, as a result of his A-ing. This establishes that an agent with the power to A-rather-than-not must have the capacity for *preference*, as opposed to mere desire: one can desire something solely because of its features considered by themselves, but one can prefer something only if one desires it in part because of the comparison between its features and those of something else to which it is preferred. The action of the agent who As-rather-than-not counts as the act that it is only because he compares it with an alternative that it excludes, and elects it over that alternative. It is possible, then, that (2.3) derives its appeal from the thought that to act on preference requires a will.

We might think that one needs a will to act on preference because one needs a will to act on desire, and preference is a species of desire. Reid identifies two differences between volition and desire:

[W]hat we will must be an action, and our own action; what we desire may not be our own action, it may be no action at all.   (*EAP* II. 1, p. 60/532*a*)

With regard to our own action, we may desire what we do not will, and will what we do not desire; nay, what we have a great aversion to.   (*EAP* II. 1, p. 61/532*a*)[13]

The fact that what we will and what we desire may conflict derives from the fact that we are committed to what we will in a manner in which we remain uncommitted to what we desire. To will something is to be determined to make it so, while to desire the very same act might involve no such determination. One might think, then, that the driving idea behind premise (2.3) is this: to act on the basis of a preference, one must be committed to so acting; but such commitment requires more than preference, since preference is a species of mere desire; the will supplies the needed commitment to action. However, the fact that this line of thought doesn't depend on the difference between preference and volition, *per se*, but only on the difference between desire, in general, and volition, counts against it. After all, this line of thought, if successful, could be offered without any appeal to the power to act-rather-than-not; any power to act would do since to have any power to act is to have a capacity that could not be exhausted by desire, on this line of thought. Thus, it could be offered

[13] Both of these points are made explicitly by Locke (*Essay Concerning Human Understanding*, II. XXI. 30). See also *TAC*, 141.

without any appeal to premises (2.1) and (2.2). Premises (2.1) and (2.2) serve to substantiate the claim that an agent who has the power to act at all must have the power to act on the basis of a preference for the act *over incompatible alternatives*. (2.3) then makes a connection between action on the basis of preference and volition. So, if we are to capture the spirit of Reid's argument from the power to do otherwise, what we need is some explanation for that connection that distinguishes it from whatever connection there might be between action on the basis of desire, on the one hand, and volition, on the other.

Reid is clear that to act on the basis of preference, rather than on the basis of desire, requires reason:

The ultimate object of [the rational] principle is what we judge to be good upon the whole. This is not the object of any of our animal principles, they being all directed to particular objects, *without any comparison with others*, or any consideration of their being good or ill upon the whole. (*EAP* III. 3. iii, p. 214/583*b*–584*a*; my emphasis)

Our judgment that a particular course of conduct tends to our good upon the whole is a reflective preference. We reach such a judgment by comparing the various goods promised by various alternative actions, and weighing them with respect to each other. To act on such a judgment is to perform one act rather than another, for it is to sacrifice the goods promised by another course of conduct for the sake of those judged to be superior. To act in this way is to act on the dictates of practical reasoning (cf. *EAP* III. 3. ii, p. 208/581*b*–582*a*).

Notice that the kind of preference of interest here should be distinguished from another sort. A person might be said to prefer x to y just because his desire for x is stronger than his desire for y. However, the preference for x over y had by the person who *judges* x, and not y, to promise his good on the whole need not be aligned with his desires: "[I]n innumerable cases in common life, our animal principles draw us one way, while a regard to what is good on the whole, draws us the contrary way. Thus the flesh lusteth against the spirit, and spirit against the flesh, and these two are contrary" (*EAP* III. 3. ii, p. 207/581*b*). While one might judge that the way of the spirit, and not that of the flesh, promises one's good upon the whole, it does not follow that one's desire for the way of the spirit is stronger than one's desire for the way of the flesh. It follows, then, that a person who has the power to A-rather-than-not has the capacity to act on a preference for A, even if the desire for not A is far stronger than the desire for A. That is, such a person has the capacity to act on the dictates of practical reason, quite independently of the dictates of desire. It is a very short step from here to the will. To direct oneself in accordance with the demands of reason just is to choose, or to will. And so we have reached an argument for (2.3):

(2.3i) If S has the power to A-rather-than-not, then S has the power to act in accordance with a judgment to the effect that A-ing, rather than not A-ing, will contribute to his good upon the whole.

(2.3ii) If S has the power to act in accordance with a judgment to the effect that A-ing, rather than not A-ing, will contribute to his good upon the whole, then S has the power to A even if his strongest desire favors his not A-ing.

(2.3iii) If S has the power to A even if his strongest desire favors his not A-ing, then S has the power to direct his conduct in accordance with the dictates of reason.

(2.3iv) If S has the power to direct his conduct in accordance with the dictates of reason, then S has a will.

∴ If S has the power to A-rather-than-not, then S has a will. (Premise (2.3))

This argument depends upon a particular way of understanding what it is to perform one act rather than another incompatible with it. The argument rests, that is, on a conception of such action as ultimately motivated by preferences that are not simply the upshot of desires with relative strengths. These are preferences that cannot be had by creatures lacking the capacity to compare goods with each other. Such comparison requires the ability to judge, and thus requires the capacity for rationality (cf. *EIP* VI. 1, p. 422). But the will is the power by virtue of which we direct ourselves in accordance with judgment. The will just is rationality's practical instrument.

Conclusion

In Reid's argument from the power to do otherwise, the will is seen as the necessary tool for the employment of power. With powers come options. When you have a power, what happens is up to you; with power comes the power to prevent. As we've seen, this commits Reid to analyzing examples, like Locke's example of the man in the locked room, in a particular way.

He must say that the question of whether or not an agent has the power to act as he behaves turns on the question of whether or not some other efficient cause assures that he will behave that way regardless of what he makes an effort to do. With powers come options in part because those who exercise their powers are not at the same time swept along by the exercise of the powers of others.

But Reid also thinks that with options comes the power to close off a path through performance of one's action. If it is up to you which way things go, then you have the power to make things go one way simply so that they won't go the other; with the power to do otherwise, comes the power to act in one way rather than another. But the power to take what one prevents from happening by acting *as* one's reason to so act requires a capacity to weigh alternatives with one another and thereby to form preferences among courses of action that may be desired to degrees that do not match one's preferential rankings. Such a power, that is, requires the capacity to reason, to weigh, and to direct one's conduct in accordance with the outcome of such weighing. The will, then, is what one needs in order to solve the problem posed by the openness of our future, a problem that we face by virtue of being endowed with powers to act.

3

From Change to Power

If the arguments discussed in Chapters 1 and 2 are successful, then only an entity capable of consciously *aiming* at an end can be endowed with power. What this implies is that power is, essentially, teleological. To banish teleology—to paint a picture of nature as devoid of ends—as the proponents of the "modern philosophy" were wont to do, is to thereby banish power; if nowhere in nature are there to be found things that aim and direct events for their own purposes, then nowhere in nature is power to be found. Not surprisingly, Reid holds the opposite view: he thinks, instead, that not only are some changes brought about by an entity that has power to produce them, but every change that occurs is brought about by an entity endowed with active power. All changes, then, serve the ends of some creature.

It is important to distinguish the claim that every event has an efficient cause (that is, that every event springs either mediately or immediately from the exertion of some creature's power to produce it) from the more familiar claim that all events have a physical cause (that is, that every event occurs in accordance with laws linking it to prior events). The claim of universal efficient causation and the claim of universal physical causation are not, prima facie, equivalent. For all that has been said, the former could be false while the latter true: to say so would be to say that every event occurs in accordance with laws linking it to prior events, and yet there are no entities in the universe endowed with active power. (Reid often interprets Hume as holding this position (cf. *EIP* VI. 6, p. 500).) Conversely, for all that has been said, there could be universal efficient causation without universal physical causation: to say so would be to say that every event springs from the exercise of power, and yet nothing occurs in accordance with laws. The laws, for Reid, are simply the rules by which efficient causes choose to act; the laws, that is, tell us how the efficient causes are resolved to exercise their power. So, power is prior to law. Were the efficient causes capricious, there would be no laws, no regularities, to be found in nature. The result would be that while every event has an efficient cause, not all events have a physical cause. As it happens, however, the efficient causes are not (for the most part) capricious, but ordered in their manner of employing their powers; a fact that Reid takes to be undeniable despite the fact that it is purely contingent and entirely unsupported by rational considerations.

Paradoxically, the grounds for believing that every event has an efficient cause, that Reid explicitly offers, rest in part on the contention that the claim is neither demonstrable nor supported by empirical evidence. The appearance of paradox is dispelled, however, when it is recognized that, for Reid, a belief that a particular proposition is true can be justified in at least one of three ways: the proposition can be logically deduced from propositions that are themselves justified; the proposition can be induced from, or empirically supported by propositions that are themselves justified; or the proposition is a first principle.[1] In order to claim the status of a first principle, a proposition must be accepted "naturally" and non-inferentially. If a proposition is accepted naturally, then human beings believe the proposition simply because they are human beings; belief in the proposition simply comes with a human constitution. To say that a proposition is a first principle is *not* to claim that it cannot, even in principle, be either deductively demonstrated or given adequate support by empirical evidence. It is quite possible that many first principles are also deductively or inductively provable. However, if the proposition is a first principle, it is not *accepted* on the basis of an inference that mirrors the steps of whatever deductive or inductive proof of it can be produced. The justification that Reid offers for the belief in universal efficient causation is, simply, that the proposition is a first principle.

Not just in the case of universal efficient causation, but in the case of many other first principles also, Reid's case for the claim that the proposition in question is a first principle has two phases. In the first, he argues that all known efforts to justify the proposition either deductively or inductively fail; in the second, he argues that, nonetheless, human beings naturally accept the proposition. Neither phase establishes much by itself. The

---

[1] There is a question as to why belief in a first principle should be justified just by virtue of the fact that the proposition in question is a first principle. Discussion of this issue would take us too far afield. For a helpful recent examination of the matter see Philip de Bary, *Thomas Reid and Scepticism: His Reliabilist Response* (London: Routledge, 2002).

failure of all deductive and inductive arguments for a claim is compatible with the claim being false, not to mention failing to be a first principle. Further, even if the proposition could be supported deductively or inductively it would not follow that it was not a first principle; deductively or inductively supportable propositions might not be accepted on the basis of that support. The second phase is similarly insubstantial when taken by itself. The fact that a proposition is accepted naturally is compatible with it being accepted on either deductive or inductive grounds: it could be that, by nature, we are led to engage in the relevant form of deductive or inductive reasoning.[2] Together, however, the two phases of argument make plausible the claim that the proposition in question is a first principle: it would be strange if the deductive or inductive arguments for a proposition that we accept naturally, on either deductive or inductive grounds, were hidden from view.

Against Demonstrations

Reid takes Hume to have shown (*Treatise of Human Nature*, I. 3. iii) that every known effort to demonstrate the claim that every event has an efficient cause fails (*EIP* VI. 6, p. 498).[3] At that point in the *Treatise*, Hume has not told us what the term "cause" means—he has not told us from what impression the idea the word expresses is copied—and so it is somewhat unclear what proposition he is claiming the arguments he attacks to be arguments for. Is he attacking purported demonstrations of the claim that every event has an efficient cause, or of the claim that every event has a physical cause? If Hume's theory of meaning—his view that all words express ideas and all ideas are copied from impressions—is read very strictly, then in *Treatise*, I. 3. iii, it must be the claim of universal physical

---

[2] It is this sense of the term "natural" to which Hume alludes when he writes: "Mankind is an inventive species; and where an invention is obvious and absolutely necessary, it may as properly be said to be natural as any thing that proceeds immediately from original principles, without the intervention of thought or reflexion" (*Treatise of Human Nature*, III. 2. i, p. 484).

[3] It is clear from context that Reid has the claim of universal efficient causation, and not universal physical causation in mind. In the course of his discussion, for instance, he writes, "The only experience we can have of [causation], is in the consciousness we have of exerting some power in ordering our thoughts and actions" (*EIP* VI. 6, p. 499). Since physical causation involves neither power nor exertion, he must be referring here to efficient causation. In addition, the causal maxim under discussion in *EIP* VI. 6 is clearly thought by Reid to be true, while he denies that all events are physically caused on the grounds that there are miracles (cf. *EAP* IV. 9, pp. 330–1/625b).

causation that is under discussion. After all, one might say, the term "cause" just means physical cause—it is the impression of constant conjunction, or perhaps the impression of the movement of the mind instilled through observation of constant conjunction, from which the idea is copied—and so one who says "Every event has a cause", intending the word "cause" to express the idea of efficient causation, speaks nonsense; there simply is no such idea. It hardly requires argument to establish that a nonsense statement is not demonstrable, and so Hume must be attacking purported demonstrations of the claim that every event has a physical cause. Reid, however, would be making a sloppy mistake if he were to read Hume in this way. Reid is busy trying to establish that the claim that every event has an *efficient* cause is a first principle, and towards that aim it would do no good to cite another philosopher's successful efforts to show the failure of putative demonstrations of an entirely different claim.

Instead, Reid must take Hume to have shown, in *Treatise*, I. 3. iii, the failure of all known efforts to demonstrate the claim that all events have an efficient cause.[4] The question of whether or not Hume has shown the failure of demonstrations of the claim of universal efficient causation depends, in turn, on whether or not the purported demonstrations to which he objects—those offered by Hobbes, Clarke, and Locke—are meant to establish that claim or something closer to the claim of universal physical causation. Hobbes's argument is particularly interesting in this regard. He writes:

[T]hat a man cannot imagine anything to begin without a cause, can no other way be made known, but by trying how he can imagine it; but if he try, he shall find as much reason, if there be no cause of the thing, to conceive it should begin at one time as another, that he hath equal reason to think it should begin at all times, which is impossible, and therefore he must think there was some special cause why it began then, rather than sooner or later; or else that it began never, but was eternal. (*Works of Thomas Hobbes*, iv. 276)[5]

---

[4] Interpreting Hume as attacking demonstrations of the claim of universal efficient causation in *Treatise*, I. 3. iii, requires ascribing Hume with a subtler theory of meaning than the theory that says that speech is nonsense when what it expresses is not an idea copied from an impression. An alternative interpretation must take the imagination to provide some content to thoughts that is not provided by the copying of impressions. For discussion, see Galen Strawson, *The Secret Connexion: Causation, Realism and David Hume* (Oxford: Clarendon Press, 1989), esp. pp. 102–8, 118–34; John Wright, *The Sceptical Realism of David Hume* (Minneapolis: University of Minnesota Press, 1983), esp. pp. 151–5.

[5] Clarke was fond of this argument. He echoes it in order to show that motion cannot "exist necessarily of itself" (*Works*, iv. 735).

We might summarize the driving idea of this argument, in broad strokes, like this: if an event's uncaused, then something's unintelligible (namely why it occurred when it did); but nothing's unintelligible, so nothing's uncaused. Hume responds:

I ask, is there any more difficulty in supposing the time and place to be fixed without a cause, than to suppose the existence to be determined in that manner? The first question that occurs on this subject is always, whether the object shall exist or not: the next, when and where it shall begin to exist. If the removal of a cause be intuitively absurd in the one case, it must be so in the other; and if that absurdity be not clear without a proof in the one case, it will equally require one in the other. The absurdity then of the one supposition can never be a proof of that of the other; since they are both upon the same footing, and must stand or fall by the same reasoning. (*Treatise of Human Nature*, I. 3. iii, p. 80)

Hume's objection is that Hobbes's argument employs its conclusion as one of its premises: it can only be shown that there is absurdity in the idea of an object that begins to exist without a cause if it is already assumed that there is an absurdity in the idea of an object beginning to exist *at a particular time* without a cause; but the latter idea is absurd only if we already accept that the idea of an uncaused event is an absurdity.

Hobbes's argument employs the Principle of Sufficient Reason; but this only implies that the argument involves the mistake Hume identifies if the Principle of Sufficient Reason is to be equated with the claim the argument intends to establish. In developing this point it will help to have Hobbes's argument set out as a *reductio ad absurdum* like so:

(3.1) Something, E, begins to exist without being caused to begin to exist. (the negation of the claim to be established)

(3.2) So, there is no reason why E should begin to exist at any one time rather than another.

(3.3) So, E exists at all times, or else there is some fact about E (namely the time at which it began to exist) for which there is no sufficient reason.

(3.4) If E began to exist, then E does not exist at all times.

(3.5) So, there is a fact for which there is no sufficient reason (namely that E began to exist at whatever time it began to exist).

(3.6) There is a sufficient reason for every fact. (Principle of Sufficient Reason)

∴ (3.1) is false; that is, everything that begins to exist has a cause of its existence.

For Hume's criticism of Hobbes's argument to be successful, (3.6) and the conclusion of the argument must be logically equivalent. That is, the claim that Hobbes is intending to establish must be the Principle of Sufficient Reason. But then Hume's criticism only provides what Reid requires if the claim of universal efficient causation is to be equated with the Principle of Sufficient Reason. If the Principle of Sufficient Reason is taken to be equivalent to the claim of universal physical causation, for instance, then Hume's criticism will have traction against Hobbes's argument only if the argument is intended to establish that very claim; but if that were so, then the fact that Hobbes's argument fails would be of little importance to Reid for its failure would not show that the claim of universal *efficient* causation did not admit of demonstration. Only if the Principle of Sufficient Reason is interpreted as equivalent to the claim of universal efficient causation will Hume have shown that Hobbes's purported demonstration "take[s] for granted the thing to be proved" (*EIP* VI. 6, p. 498) in a way which helps Reid's cause.

Reid discusses the Principle of Sufficient Reason in the *Essays on the Active Powers*. His concern there is with the role that the principle is put in "arguments for necessity", and so he is concerned with the question "[W]as there a sufficient reason for [each voluntary] action or not?" (*EAP* IV. 9, p. 329/625a). Reid answers by arguing that, depending on how the question is understood, the answer is either "no", or, if the answer is "yes", no damage is done to the position of those who think human beings have active power. To this end, he identifies three different ways in which the question can be understood: "[W]as there a motive to the action sufficient to justify it to be wise and good, or at least, innocent? . . . [W]as there a cause [that is, an efficient cause] of the action? . . . [W]as there something previous to the action, which made it to be necessarily produced?" (*EAP* IV. 9, p. 329/625a–b). The three questions identified here correspond to three different interpretations of the Principle of Sufficient Reason. Of these three, it is only if the principle is given the second interpretation—under which the principle is equated with the claim that every event has an efficient cause—that Hobbes's argument assumes what Reid must think it aims to prove (namely, that every event has an efficient cause). However, Reid thinks that taken in either of the other two senses the Principle of Sufficient Reason is false. Many things are not motivated in some way that serves to show them to be "wise and good", and many events—in particular free human actions—are not "necessarily produced". Here an event is thought to be "necessarily produced" when it is not efficiently caused by the creature to whom it is happening (cf. *EAP* IV. 1, p. 259/599*b*); my falling would be necessarily produced, for instance, if I was pushed. But it is false, Reid thinks, to say that every event is necessarily produced; many events are caused by the very same creature to whom they are happening. Thus, Reid would say that premise (3.6) of Hobbes's argument either amounts to the argument's conclusion, or else is false.

Reid does consider a fourth possible interpretation of the Principle of Sufficient Reason:

> When we say that a philosopher has assigned a sufficient reason for . . . a phenomenon, what is the meaning of this? The meaning surely is, that he has accounted for it from the known laws of nature. The sufficient reason of a phenomenon of nature must therefore be some law or laws of nature, of which the phenomenon is a necessary consequence. (*EAP* IV. 9, p. 330/625*b*)

Understood in this way, the Principle of Sufficient Reason is equivalent to the claim that every event is physically caused: to give a reason is just to subsume under a law; but those events that are subsumable under laws are just those that are physically caused. Although Reid expresses doubt that this is true (on the grounds that there are miracles (*EAP* IV. 9, pp. 330–1/ 625*b*)), when the principle is so interpreted, Hobbes's argument does seem to presuppose its conclusion. Or, rather, it does so when a suppressed premise of the argument is identified. The suppressed premise is the premise that makes it possible to deduce (3.2) from (3.1). For this inference to go through, we need a claim such as the following:

(3.1*a*) If an event is uncaused, then there is no reason for it.

(3.1*a*) might be thought true for the following reason: to give a reason for an event is to subsume the event under a law; but an uncaused event is an event that cannot be subsumed under a law. When his argument is interpreted so as to include premise (3.1*a*), Hobbes begins by noting that an uncaused event is an event that can't be subsumed under a law; this is then taken to be an absurd conclusion on the grounds that all events are subsumable under laws. If the conclusion of the argument is the claim that every event is physically caused, then Hobbes is reasoning in a circle. On the other hand, if the conclusion is the claim that every event is efficiently caused, then the conclusion doesn't follow from the premises.

So, if the Principle of Sufficient Reason is understood as either the claim that every event comes about for some wise and good purpose, or as the claim that every event is caused by something other than the entity to which it occurs, then the principle is false. On the other hand, if the Principle of Sufficient Reason is understood as either the claim that every event is efficiently caused or the claim that every event is physically caused then, indeed, Hobbes is arguing in a circle just as Hume contends and Reid endorses. But it is not clear that the principle needs to be interpreted in any of these four ways. Reid fails to mention explicitly yet another possible interpretation of the Principle of Sufficient Reason. Instead of claiming that all events are well-motivated, the principle might claim just that all events are motivated, whether well or ill. That is, the principle can be taken to be saying that every event is end-directed: every event is either a means to some agent's end, or else its occurrence is, itself, some agent's end. The ends that the event serves might be evil, absurd, or in some other way unjustifiable.

When the Principle of Sufficient Reason is so understood, Hobbes's argument does not assume what it aims to prove. Under this interpretation, Reid would be committed to denying that the Principle of Sufficient Reason is equivalent to the claim of universal efficient causation. By producing arguments for the claim that active power presupposes will and understanding, and thus committing himself to the claim that all efficiently caused events are end-directed, Reid would be committing himself to denying that it is all one to claim that all events are end-directed and to claim that they are all efficiently caused. It requires demonstrative argument to show that all efficiently caused events are end-directed; that fact is accepted on the basis of reason and, therefore, is no first principle.

When the Principle of Sufficient Reason is interpreted as claiming that all events are end-directed, Hobbes's argument only succeeds when it is assumed that every end-directed event is efficiently caused. Without that assumption, (3.2) does not follow from (3.1). This would amount to assuming the argument's conclusion, if the claim were rooted in the proposition that all events, whether or not end-directed, are efficiently caused. However, the claim need not be so rooted. Instead, the claim could be understood as forging a link between efficient causation and teleological intelligibility; this link is then exploited in order to establish universal efficient causation by the claim that all events are intelligible as either means or ends. But what grounds are there for believing that all end-directed events are efficiently caused? One might think that an event cannot be end-directed unless some creature has the end in question—actually intends to bring about that end. But it doesn't follow from that that the creature who intends the end is the efficient cause of the end-directed event.

From Change to Power · 65

Perhaps, for instance, the event is physically caused by the mental state of intending the end and not efficiently caused by anything at all. As we will see, Reid has an argument for the claim that all end-directed events are efficiently caused by the creature who has the end in question. (Reid's discussion of this claim and his grounds for holding it will be postponed until Chapter 4.)

The important point here, however, is this: Reid cannot reject Hobbes's argument on the grounds provided by Hume. When the Principle of Sufficient Reason is interpreted as the claim that all events are end-directed, then Reid himself is committed to the argument that Hobbes provides. Reid holds that all events are end-directed, and he holds that every end-directed event is efficiently caused by the being whose end the event serves. These two claims together commit him to a demonstrative argument for the claim that every event is efficiently caused. This fact does not, by itself, vitiate Reid's contention that the proposition asserting universal efficient causation is a first principle; the fact, after all, that a claim is demonstrable does not imply that the claim is accepted through an inference that mirrors the demonstration for it. However, his case for thinking universal efficient causation to be a first principle is nonetheless weakened by his own commitment to a providential picture of the universe, a picture in which each change unfolds for the sake of the ends of some entity with power to produce it.

Against Inductive Arguments

Reid offers two reasons for denying the claim that there is empirical support for universal efficient causation.[6] One reason he offers is that the only events that we know from observation to be efficiently caused are our own actions (a claim discussed in Chapter 1), and since our actions make up such a tiny percentage of all events, it is not a sufficient base from which to draw the general conclusion (*EIP* VI. 6, p. 499). Reid's other reason, however, is more philosophically interesting. He expresses it as follows:

[T]he proposition to be proved, is not a contingent, but a necessary proposition. It is not, that things which begin to exist commonly have a cause, or even that they

---

[6] He offers three remarks in this context (*EIP* VI. 6, pp. 498–9), but the second of them amounts to claiming only that people have not, in fact, based their belief in the universality of efficient causation on observation. If true, this claim provides direct support for the claim that the proposition is a first principle, as opposed to the indirect support provided by arguments to the effect that efforts to empirically support the proposition fail.

always in fact have a cause; but that they must have a cause, and cannot begin to exist without a cause.

Propositions of this kind, from their nature, are incapable of proof by induction. Experience informs us only of what is, or has been, not of what must be; and the conclusion must be of the same nature with the premises.   (*EIP* IV. 6, p. 498; see also *EAP* I. 5, p. 39/524*b*)

It can be argued that Reid is making a simple modal error. He seems to be arguing that the following proposition cannot be given empirical support:

> *Universal Necessity of Efficient Causation*: For every event, it is necessarily the case that that event is efficiently caused. That is: $\forall(e)(\Box C(e))$

Although Reid does not mention it, this proposition is to be contrasted with the following:

> *Necessity of Universal Efficient Causation*: It is necessarily the case that every event is efficiently caused. That is: $\Box\forall(e)(C(e))$

Reid's point is that to provide empirical support for the first of these principles, the Universal Necessity of Efficient Causation, one would have to observe not just what is, in fact, the case, but also what must be the case. He seems to think that empirical support for the Universal Necessity of Efficient Causation requires observation of more than the fact that a particular event has an efficient cause; it also requires observation of the necessity of that fact. Since we cannot observe necessity, we cannot have any observational evidence for the Universal Necessity of Efficient Causation. This line of thought depends upon a simple conception of the conditions under which an observation provides support for a universal generalization: an observation provides support for a universal generalization just in case the observation is of one of the instances of the generalization.

If we allow this very simple construal of the conditions under which observations support universal generalizations, there is a problem with this line of reasoning. The problem is that in standard modal logics the Universal Necessity of Efficient Causation is equivalent to the Necessity of Universal Efficient Causation: to say that all events are a certain way in all possible worlds is the same as to say that in all possible worlds all events are a certain way. However, given the very simple construal of the conditions under which an observation supports a universal generalization, there do not seem to be any principled grounds for denying that the Necessity of Universal Efficient Causation can be empirically supported, even if the support that can be provided for it is quite weak. In the passage just quoted,

Reid seems to admit that we could have empirical support for the claim that what begins to exist always in fact has a cause; that is, he admits that there could be empirical support for the claim that every actual event is, in fact, efficiently caused. If we conceive of necessity as truth in all possible worlds, then it would seem that we can have empirical support for a claim of necessity in the same way that we can have empirical support for any other universal generalization: by observation of one of the generalization's instances—in this case, by observation of one of the many possible worlds (namely, the actual world) within the scope of the universal quantifier ranging over all possible worlds.

What this line of reasoning shows, however, is that there is something wrong with the view that an observation supports a universal generalization just in case it is an observation of one of the generalization's instances. We cannot generalize from the nature of the actual world to the nature of possible worlds. The obstacle does not come from the fact that we can only observe one of the many possible worlds—even one conforming observation supplies some, albeit weak, empirical support to a universal generalization—but rather from the fact that no principle of uniformity seems to extend from the actual to the possible in the way that such a principle does extend from the past to the future. It is the fact that we are unjustified in expecting the possible to be like the actual that is fueling the first of Reid's arguments against the claim that universal efficient causation can be empirically supported.

It is worth noting that, although this must be what Reid has in mind, it is inconsistent with his official account of necessity and contingency. He writes: "Contingent truths are . . . mutable, they may be true at one time, and not at another; and therefore the expression of them must include some point or period of time" (*EIP* VI. 5, p. 469). If we take Reid to be implying that a truth is necessary just in case it is true at all times and places, then there is no reason whatsoever to think that a necessary truth couldn't be given empirical support: to provide it, one merely needs to travel from place to place at different times and see if the proposition is true. However, Reid's remark here hardly reaches the nature of contingency. If he is understood to be claiming that contingent truths are, in fact, false at some time, then all true propositions that happen to be always true—such as time-indexed truths—will turn out to be necessary, which is an unsatisfactory result. On the other hand, if, as the text seems to suggest, the remark is to be understood as claiming that contingent truths are truths that *could be* false at some particular time, then the appeal to time is doing no work, and the test is uninformative: what makes some truth contingent is just that it could be false. In fact, Reid's official definition of necessity and contingency is something of a muddle, and it does not seem to inform his argument against the claim that universal efficient causation can be empirically supported, an argument that should be understood as marking the difficulty in generalizing from the way things are to the way they could be and taking observation to tell us only about the way things are.

The Natural, Uninferred Belief

Reid often contends that the proof that human beings naturally and non-inferentially believe in universal efficient causation is that conduct in which we commonly engage is rational, or justified, only if every event has an efficient cause, and we engage in such conduct even in the absence of anything that would serve as an argument for the claim. Here is one typical statement of this contention:

> Suppose a man's house to be broken open, his money and jewels taken away: such things have happened times innumerable without any apparent cause; and were he only to reason from experience in such a case, how must he behave? He must put in one scale the instances wherein a cause was found of such an event, and in the other scale, the instances wherein no cause was found, and the preponderant scale must determine, whether it be most probable that there was a cause of this event, or that there was none. Would any man of common understanding have recourse to such an expedient to direct his judgment? (*EIP* VI. 6, p. 502)

In the case that Reid imagines, not only does the man have no good argument for the claim that there is some cause of his misfortune, but he seems to have inductive evidence to the contrary: there are far more events for which he knows no cause than there are events for which he knows a cause. However, as it stands, the example is in need of much more support than Reid provides, if it is to illustrate the point that he takes it to illustrate. It is undeniable that in calling the police, or launching a vendetta, the man is assuming that there is some cause, in *some* sense of the term, of his suffering. Further, it is undeniable that to suggest that the man believes this on the basis of some deductive or inductive argument is to ascribe him with more than one thought too many. But these facts are just as easily accounted for by appeal to the naturalness of an uninferred belief that every event has a *physical* cause as they are by appeal to a natural and uninferred belief in universal *efficient* causation. In fact, arguably anyway, they are accounted for better by appeal to belief in universal physical causation than in efficient. If the man has never heard of any human being stealing from any other, he may think it more likely that a tornado broke down his door and whisked his things away than did another person. The tornado is no efficient cause—it doesn't have a mind—but it is a possible physical cause; it is a place in which events could take place that are conjoined by law with the loss of the man's property. So, it seems that the man naturally assumes his misfortune to be physically caused but does not naturally assume that his misfortune serves the ends of some other creature, independently of experience with the venality of others. Therefore, it is far from clear that he naturally and non-inferentially assumes that the events have an efficient cause in Reid's sense.

Seemingly incongruously, with almost as much regularity as he insists that the rationality of our everyday behavior presupposes belief in universal efficient causation, Reid insists that efficient causes are almost never relevant to ordinary practices but that the existence only of *physical* causes is what we rely upon in our ordinary behavior. For instance, he writes:

To know the event and the circumstances that attended it, and to know in what circumstances like events may be expected, may be of consequence in the conduct of life; but to know the real efficient, whether it be matter or mind, whether of a superior or inferior order, concerns us little. (*EAP* I. 5, p. 33/522*b*; see also *EAP* IV. 3, p. 279/607*a; TAC* 190)

Reid does temper this conclusion with the suggestion that our moral practices—the assessing of the responsibility of others and ourselves, the meting out of praise and blame, the giving and receiving of promises—depend upon a presumption of efficient causality, even if knowledge of the "real efficient" is irrelevant for other purposes.[7] However, tempering the conclusion in this way doesn't mute the primary point that Reid is making: our practices don't in general require that we know the efficient causes of events; at most, that we should know the efficient cause of every *morally relevant* event is all that our practices require. Even the examples—such as the example just discussed of the man who finds his house robbed—that

---

[7] This claim can be questioned. Is it so clear that justifiably morally to blame a person for events in which he engages, for instance, requires justifiably holding that person to be the efficient cause of the events in question, or are certain forms of physical causation (by mental states of the person, for instance) sufficient to justify moral censure? These issues are discussed at greater length in Ch. 4 in connection with Reid's account of character traits.

Reid explicitly claims to illustrate our tacit belief in universal efficient causation, at best only illustrate the weaker claim that we assume that all *morally relevant* events are efficiently caused.[8]

There is a temptation to see Reid as holding fundamentally inconsistent views about precisely what belief it is to which we are committed in our practices. He seems to be unconsciously vacillating between three views: the view that we naturally and non-inferentially believe in universal efficient causation, the view that we naturally and non-inferentially believe in the efficient causation of all morally relevant events, and the view that we naturally and non-inferentially believe in universal physical causation. The third of these claims, and not the first, is consistent with Reid's view that efficient causes are irrelevant to the guidance of ordinary, prudential conduct (avoiding the hot stove, for instance), while at best only the second claim is illustrated by the examples that he adduces that are intended to illustrate our tacit belief.

However, this portrait of Reid as swinging wildly among these various possible interpretations of the belief in the universality of causation can be avoided. We can avoid this picture by ascribing to Reid the following view. One event physically causes another only if the physical effect is efficiently caused. That is, there is no physical causation without efficient. If Reid holds this, then his view that we all naturally believe in universal efficient causation can be made consistent with his view that the rationality of our non-moral conduct requires guidance by beliefs regarding physical causes, but not by beliefs regarding efficient. If one cannot rationally believe all events to be physically caused without believing them to be efficiently caused, and if our ordinary practices are rational only if guided by the former belief and sometimes (in the case of moral practices) by the latter, then our ordinary practices are rational only if guided by the belief in universal efficient causation.

And, in fact, Reid does hold that one event physically causes another only if there is an efficient cause behind the transaction. He writes:

I think... that every physical cause must be the work of some agent or efficient cause. Thus, that a body put in motion continues to move till it be stopped, is an effect which, for what I know, may be owing to an inherent property in matter;

---

[8] The puzzling nature of Reid's grounds for thinking that we all naturally and non-inferentially believe all events to be efficiently caused is discussed in R. F. Stalley, "Causality and Agency in the Philosophy of Thomas Reid", in M. Dalgarno and E. Matthews (eds.), *The Philosophy of Thomas Reid* (Dordrecht: Kluwer Academic Publishers, 1989), 278–82. The solution to the puzzle offered here is closely related to Stalley's solution.

if this be so, this property of matter is the physical cause of the continuance of the motion; but the ultimate efficient cause is the Being who gave this property to matter. (COR 111, p. 206)

Reid holds this view for reasons the appreciation of which requires further examination of his view of efficient causality, and the problem about causation that he inherits from Hume.

To see this, start with a famous passage from Hume's *Enquiry*. Hume writes:

The bread, which I formerly eat, nourished me; that is, a body of such sensible qualities, was, at that time, endowed with such secret powers: But does it follow, that other bread must also nourish me at another time, and that like sensible qualities must always be attended with like secret powers? The consequence seems nowise necessary. At least, it must be acknowledged, that there is here a consequence drawn by the mind; that there is a certain step taken; a process of thought, and an inference, which wants to be explained... These two propositions are far from being the same, *I have found that such an object has always been attended with such an effect*, and *I foresee, that other objects, which are, in appearance, similar, will be attended with similar effects.* I shall allow, if you please, that the one proposition may justly be inferred from the other: I know in fact, that it always is inferred. But if you insist, that the inference is made by a chain of reasoning, I desire you to produce that reasoning. (*Enquiry Concerning Human Understanding*, IV. 2, p. 34)

Hume is paving the way for an argument of the following form:

- I infer that a like event to that which I observed in the past will follow on the occurrence of an event like that which I observed in the past to precede it.
- In drawing this inference, I do not employ reason.
- ∴ The inference takes place through custom or habit.

Reid accepts the premises, but rejects the conclusion, for he thinks that there is a third way in which the inference can proceed: through an inferential process that we engage in because of the way in which we are built and on which we cannot but rely. That is, in relying on our tendency to make inferences on the basis of past experience—to employ what Reid calls "the inductive principle" (*INQ* 6. 24, p. 199)—is not to employ reason, nor is it to be in the grip of an acquired habit; it is, instead, a principle of inference embedded in our constitution as human beings.

So far there is little of substance with which Hume would disagree. Hume accepts Locke's anti-nativism according to which mental capacities are never thought native if their functioning can be explained through the influence of experience; explanations in terms of the influence of experience take precedence over nativist appeals. So Hume would be quick to worry that Reid is simply asserting our tendency to make inductive inferences to be native, while it is possible to explain how we come to have this tendency through experience.[9] But Hume himself doesn't argue for his anti-nativist views, but (with a nod to Locke) simply takes them for granted, and so he is not likely to see Reid's assertion that we all naturally rely on the inductive principle to amount to meaningful engagement with anything for which he has produced argument. However, and this is the important point on which Hume and Reid differ, we can also be confident, Reid thinks, that the inferential principle on which we are justified in relying is *grounded* in the metaphysical facts: there is indeed something in nature which insures that like events will be followed by like events.[10] What could that "something" be? The answer is power and a tendency to exert it in a consistent manner. In being confident that like will follow like we are being confident of two things: first, that where there is likeness in all observable respects to what we have seen in the past there is likeness, also, in *power*; and second, that where there is a past pattern of performance there is a *resolution* on the part of the entity with power to try to behave in a similar way in similar circumstances.

The view just sketched is intertwined with Reid's view of laws of nature. He frequently suggests that laws of nature should be understood simply as patterns in the conduct of efficient causes. For instance,

Even the great Bacon seems to have thought that there is a *latens processus*, as he calls it, *by which* natural causes really produce their effects; and that, in the progress of philosophy, this might be discovered. But Newton, more enlightened on this point, has taught us to acquiesce in *a law of nature, according to which* the effect is produced, as the utmost that natural philosophy can reach, leaving what can be

---

[9] In fact, Hume says as much in a letter in which he comments on Reid's *Inquiry*. See, "David Hume to Hugh Blair (4 July 1762)", *INQ* 256–7. This issue is discussed in John Wright, "Hume vs. Reid on Ideas: The New Hume Letter", *Mind*, 96/383 (July 1987), 392–8.

[10] The order of Reid's inference here should be highlighted. Reid does not reason that we are justified in our inductive inferences only if physical effects are efficiently caused. Rather, he thinks that we are justified in our inductive inferences based upon the discovery of the physical causes of phenomena since in making them we employ the inductive principle, which is a first principle of our constitutions. From this he concludes that every physical effect must be efficiently caused. The inference runs from the epistemological facts to the metaphysical, rather than in the reverse direction.

known of the agent or efficient cause to metaphysicks or natural theology. This I look upon as one of the great discoveries of Newton. (COR, app. A, pp. 243–4; emphasis in the original; see also TAC 183)

Reid takes Newton to have shown us that laws of nature are the rules that guide the conduct of the efficient causes of phenomenon. Given the connection that Reid makes between active power and end-directedness, it follows that the discovery of a law of nature, of the rule guiding an efficient cause's behavior, is discovery of more than just a brute fact in nature; the discovery of the laws of nature is the discovery of the ends that guide the efficient causes of change.

It is clear that Reid's appeal to power and a tendency to exert it in a uniform manner does not provide the sort of solution to the problem of induction that would satisfy Hume. Reid appeals, in essence, to another past regularity (namely, regularity in exertion of power) to justify projection of one past regularity into the future (for instance, that an unsupported object will fall). But on the tip of the tongue of any good Humean is the question of why we should be any more justified in projecting that other regularity than we are in projecting the regularity it is marshaled to support. What grounds are there for believing that powers exerted in a pattern in the past will continue to be exerted similarly in the future? Reid admits that this cannot be justified either deductively or inductively; it cannot be given justification through reason. But this does not mean that regularity in exertion is simply a lucky accident that might change at any moment. Instead, regularity in exertion comes from the fact that the entity in question is resolved to exert its powers in the future much as it has exerted them in the past. The question is, however, why the appeal to "resolution" should amount to any more than an appeal to another regularity coupled with the insistence that we can count on this one to be projectible.

It seems that Reid's best hope for avoiding this objection is to develop an account of the resolution to exert consistently under which the objection does not apply. But what is this "resolution"? If the resolution is just a temporally extended event, or persistent feature of the mind of the agent in question, then, indeed, Reid is appealing without justification to one regularity in order to justify reliance on another. So understood, he is appealing to a past constant conjunction between resolution and exertion to justify projection of the constant conjunction of, for instance, being unsupported and falling. To avoid this result, Reid must deny that the resolution of the efficient cause is related to its exertions of its power in the manner in which events are related in laws of nature. However, he cannot say that an agent has the resolution to exert itself consistently just in case it exerts itself consistently. To say that would be to provide no more of a justification of inductive inferences than Hume can provide, for under such a view, to believe the agent to have the resolution translates without remainder to the belief that the future will resemble the past. Hume thinks that we all believe *that*. The question is whether there is any feature of the world other than the fact of regularity itself that accounts for the truth of the belief; the belief in resolution fills the gap only if it is different from the belief to be justified.

The right answer to the question "What is the resolution to exert consistently?" doesn't look like an answer at all: the resolution is that in virtue of which the agent exerts itself consistently. If more could be said about the nature of the resolution, then the belief that the future will resemble the past could be justified through reason: through either some deductive or inductive link between the resolution and the consistency of behavior. By agreeing that the reliance on the inductive principle cannot be justified through reason, Reid silences the question about the nature of the resolution to exert consistently. The resolution just is the fact about the world by virtue of which we are justified in relying on the inductive principle, even if we cannot, even in principle, specify anything about that fact that illuminates the role that it plays in making it the case that the future resembles the past.

The appeal to the resolution to exert in a consistent manner, then, is just like appeals to the "nature" or "essence" of a thing in answer to regressive "why"-questioning. When we reach the end of reason-giving—when we can no longer cite one fact to explain another—we just say "That's the way things are." Hume would say this much in answer to the question of why the future resembles the past. But when asked why things are that way, Reid adds that it is in the nature of things to be that way; the efficient causes are resolved to exert themselves in the future as they have in the past. The question is whether, in offering this answer, it is possible to travel between the horns of the following dilemma: this answer either adds nothing, or else it manifests a failure to appreciate the claim that the inductive principle cannot be justified through reason. If the further appeal to "natures" is to travel between the horns of the dilemma, then it must amount to the assertion that there is something beyond our conceptions that accounts for the fact that things are that way, but accounts for it in some way entirely different from the way in which one proposition accounts for a proposition for which it provides deductive or inductive support. The resolution to exert in a consistent manner is that something; it is what makes it true that the future will resemble the past, even though it lies continually outside our capacities to appreciate how it makes that so. This is not the sort of answer to the problem of induction that would satisfy Hume. It is not just the hope, but the faith, in a metaphysics that mirrors the movements of our minds: where there is a justified inductive inference, Reid thinks, there is the push of power and a resolution to exert it in a consistent manner. But as to how this provides a solution to the problem of induction, there is nothing more to say.

Still, to say even this much is to say that behind every physical–causal interaction there is an efficient cause. We cannot help but believe this, Reid thinks, any more than we can stably maintain acceptance of a skeptical position on the problem of induction. But then in so far as our practices rely, and cannot help but rely, on the belief in universal physical causation they are guided, also, by a natural belief in universal efficient causation.

Conclusion

Reid's commitment to the claim that there is a constitutive connection between end-directedness and efficient causation (a connection to be discussed in the next chapter) commits him to acceptance of Hobbes's demonstration of universal efficient causation, and thus commits him to rejecting Hume's contention that every such putative demonstration fails. And such a commitment on his part should be no surprise. Any thinker who takes providence seriously—who believes that the world does, in fact, follow the Order of Grace—and who also takes harmony, order, and end-directedness to require authorship, is thereby committed to a demonstration of the claim that every event is efficiently caused. Since rejection of all demonstrations of the universality of efficient causation is intended only to strengthen the case for thinking our belief in it to be uninferred, but is not strictly necessary to that case, Reid is best read as committed to the view that there is a valid demonstration of the claim but that that demonstration plays no role in our acceptance of it. Reid should hold that we have a natural belief in universal efficient causation—manifested in ordinary reliance on inductive inferences and, perhaps, in moral appraisal—that is uninferred despite the fact that it could be inferred through a line of reasoning very close to that offered by Hobbes and criticized by Hume.

4
From End-Directedness to Power

In the last chapter, it was suggested that, although Reid thinks that we never reason to the conclusion that every event is efficiently caused, but simply accept it non-inferentially, he is committed to thinking that that claim can be demonstrated. The demonstration runs in two steps. First, every event serves a purpose, is directed towards an end. Second, every end-directed event is the product of some entity's exertion of its power to produce the event in question. The first of these claims is a providentialist presumption which was taken for granted by most of Reid's contemporaries (although not by Hume), and for which Reid provides no direct argument.[1] He probably believes this first claim to be as certain, and no more certain, than the claim that every event is efficiently caused.[2] Reid has much more to say with regard to the second claim, and it is that claim with which this chapter is concerned. The link that Reid forges between end-directedness and efficient causation comes out in what Reid calls the "third argument for moral liberty" (*EAP* IV. 8, pp. 321–5/622b–624a).

All three arguments for moral liberty are intended to establish not just that human behavior is efficiently caused, but that it is caused by the

---

[1] He does claim that the following is a first principle: "That design and intelligence in the cause, may with certainty be inferred from marks or signs of it in the effect" (*EIP* VI. 6, p. 509). When coupled with the claims that every event indicates intelligence, and that every event is efficiently caused, this yields the claim that all events are end-directed. However, if the claim that every event is efficiently caused is marshaled in support of the claim that every event is end-directed, then the latter cannot be employed in a demonstration of the former.

[2] Thus, he would hold that the demonstration of the claim that all events are efficiently caused just described does not serve as a *proof*, in the sense of that term discussed in the introduction.

person whose behavior it is. The arguments are intended, that is, not just to rule out the picture of the universe as devoid of power, and thus of efficient causation, but also to rule out the Malebranchian picture under which every event is efficiently caused, but no human being is the efficient cause of any event.[3] The first two arguments for moral liberty have received some discussion in recent years, in the secondary literature on Reid, but the third argument has been all but ignored. The first argument claims that only radical skepticism could lead us to reject our natural conviction that we are capable of efficiently causing our conduct, and then invokes arguments against radical skepticism to argue for the claim that the conviction is correct. The second argument claims that we are tacitly committed to the belief that human beings are the efficient causes of their conduct by our moral practices, including those of praising and blaming.

In the third argument, Reid attempts to derive the claim that human beings are the efficient causes of their actions from the fact that we are endowed with the capacity to make and execute plans. He thinks that if we make and execute plans—if our conduct, that is, is end-directed—then we are (to some degree) wise; and he thinks that any creature that is to some degree wise must be endowed with active power. Both steps are puzzling, and the few commentators who have discussed the argument have either simply evinced their own puzzlement, or else have taken the argument to be reiterating points to be found in the other two arguments for moral liberty.[4] There are two apparent problems: first, plenty of planned conduct seems

---

[3] Given that Reid holds that it is a first principle that human beings are endowed with active power, one might find it strange that he offers *arguments* for that claim. After all, first principles are never accepted on the basis of argument. However, as has been noted already, this does not imply that arguments cannot be given for first principles; they can, although those arguments do not describe the grounds on which people accept the first principles the arguments support. For an alternative way of explaining why Reid employs the three arguments for moral liberty in support of the relevant first principle, see James Harris, "On Reid's 'Inconsistent Triad': A Reply to McDermid", *British Journal for the History of Philosophy*, 11/1 (2003), 121–7.

[4] Baruch Brody, in his introduction to Reid's *Essays on the Active Powers of Man*, gives only one paragraph of discussion to the argument and dubs it "very strange" (*EAP*, p. xviii). William Rowe's book *Thomas Reid on Freedom and Morality* (Ithaca, NY: Cornell University Press, 1991) contains no discussion at all of the third argument, although Rowe does discuss the first and second arguments in detail. Edward Madden, "Common Sense and Agency Theory", *Review of Metaphysics*, 36 (1982), 319–41, discusses the argument briefly but concludes that it "adds nothing new" (p. 337). Keith Lehrer gives the argument a couple of pages of discussion in his *Thomas Reid* (London: Routledge, 1989), 276–8. I say a word more about Lehrer's thoughts on the argument in a later footnote. The best discussion of the argument to be found, although it is still far from complete, appears in Douglas McDermid's very helpful essay "Thomas Reid on Moral Liberty and Common Sense", *British Journal for the History of Philosophy*, 7/2 (1999), 275–303

to be utterly foolish; second, wisdom appears, anyway, to be a trait that could be possessed by the impotent. If wisdom is construed, for instance, as a stable disposition to act in a certain way and to have certain feelings, then it could be no different in kind from sugar's disposition to dissolve in water, or the cat's disposition to chase the moving yarn. In all three cases, we might say that the possessor of the relevant disposition is simply subject to the workings of physical causation, but is not an efficient cause of its own behavior.

However, if the third argument for moral liberty can overcome the substantial difficulties that it faces, then it can be used to support the demonstration, alluded to above, of the claim that every event is efficiently caused. While Reid seems to assume, in his presentation of the third argument, that every event is efficiently caused, the third argument nowhere depends on that claim. Further, since the argument, if it succeeds, establishes a link between end-directedness and power, it follows, given the providentialist presumption that all events are end-directed, that every event is efficiently caused.

Reid states the third argument as follows:

> [U]nderstanding without power may project, but can execute nothing. A regular plan of conduct, as it cannot be contrived without understanding, so it cannot be carried into execution without power; and, therefore, the execution, as an effect, demonstrates, with equal force, both power and understanding in the cause. Every indication of wisdom, taken from the effect, is equally an indication of power to execute what wisdom planned. And, if we have any evidence that the wisdom which formed the plan is in the man, we have the very same evidence that the power which executed it is in him also. (*EAP* IV. 8, pp. 321–2/622b)

Reid appears to be reasoning as follows:

(4.1) An individual's complex sequence of actions tending toward an end indicate that that individual is wise.

(4.2) If a sequence of actions indicates that an individual is wise, then it indicates that the individual is the efficient cause of each of the actions in the sequence.[5]

(esp. pp. 286–8). McDermid, who discusses all three of the arguments for moral liberty, offers an account of the argument that is correct, although he fails to capture, in my view, the argument's philosophical import or central presuppositions. As McDermid sees it, the argument ultimately depends on the same set of claims about the priority of common sense that drive the first argument.

[5] The consequent of this premise is intended to capture Reid's claim that the "power which executed" the plan is in the same creature who had the plan. Whether or not this is the right way to understand Reid depends on the question of what, exactly, is involved for him in the

(4.3) If an individual is the efficient cause of an action, then he has moral liberty.

∴ Those individuals who perform wise and complex sequences of actions (i.e. almost everyone) are invested with moral liberty.

Premise (4.3) follows from Reid's definition of moral liberty. An agent has moral liberty with respect to a particular act if and only if he has the power to will the act (cf. *EAP* IV. 1, p. 259/599*a–b*).[6] However, given that an agent has a power to act only if he has the power to will the act,[7] and given that an agent who is the efficient cause of an event has the power to bring the event about, it follows that an agent who is the efficient cause of an event has moral liberty with respect to it.

As we will see, both the connection postulated in premise (4.1) between end-directedness and wisdom, and the connection postulated in premise (4.2) between wisdom and power, fall out of Reid's account of character traits in general, and out of his account of the trait of wisdom, in particular. So, it is to the account of character that we turn first.

Character Traits

Reid's account of character traits begins with a taxonomy of different ways in which one can have a purpose, or, as he sometimes puts it, different ways in which one can be resolved:

Our purposes are of two kinds. We may call one *particular*, the other *general*. By a *particular* purpose, I mean that which has for its object an individual action, limited to one time and place; by a *general* purpose, that of a course or train of action, intended for some general end, or regulated by some general rule. (*EAP* II. 3, p. 84/539*b*)

execution of a plan. The formulation of premise (4.2) presupposes that to execute a plan is to be the efficient cause of each of the actions involved in carrying out the plan. Perhaps there are cases in which the execution of a plan does not require this; maybe, for instance, an agent can be the efficient cause of only some of the relevant actions and still be said to have executed the plan. In any event, whatever construal of plan execution is correct could be employed in the consequent of premise (4.2) without losing the force of the argument.

[6] Since, for Reid, the power to act in a certain way entails the power not to act that way, this definition is equivalent, for him, to the following definition: an agent has moral liberty with respect to a particular act if and only if he has the power to will the act and the power not to will the act.

[7] This is the upshot of the claims discussed in Ch. 1 to the effect that where there is power there is the power to exert, and that all exertions of power are volitions.

In drawing the distinction between particular and general purposes, Reid seems to be employing three different contrasts in the content of intentions. First, we might contrast aiming to produce a particular individual event with aiming to produce some token of an event type. We can imagine, that is, that there is no event that can be substituted for the event at which I aim and still satisfy my intention, or, alternatively, that any event belonging to a particular type will do. Second, we might contrast aiming to produce some token of an event type where the type-defining features include a particular time and place, with aiming to produce a token of an event type where the type-defining features do not include times and places. That is, we can imagine that any event of a particular sort will satisfy my intention so long as it occurs in a specific time and place, or that the time and place do not matter to me. And, third, we might contrast aiming to produce an event that serves an end quite independently of the occurrence of other events, on the one hand, with aiming to produce an event that serves an end only if it occurs as part of a "train" of events, on the other. An agent might, for instance, intend to open the door in order to create a cross-breeze and so intend even if he's never done such a thing before, never plans to do anything like it ever again, and need do nothing else to accomplish his end. By contrast, if one resolves to pay for a magazine subscription one's conduct only makes sense as part of a train of actions that includes reading the magazine when it arrives. All of the actions in the "train" are united by some principle that defines a particular type of action to which they all belong. In the simplest case, they will all belong to a type of the form "actions that further end E".

Perhaps because he takes all three contrasts to draw the lines between purposes in the same way, Reid seems to hold that a general purpose is general in all three senses: one who has a general purpose aims to produce any token of a type of event that is not time- or place-specific and the purpose is served by the event's occurrence only if there are other occurrences of events that belong to the same type. To have a general purpose, then, is to aim at a particular pattern of conduct; the pattern is the point; it is that at which the agent aims.

In addition to the distinction between general and particular purposes, Reid distinguishes two species of general purpose: those "intended for some general end" and those "regulated by some general rule". This distinction is a distinction between two different sorts of pattern that one's conduct might instantiate. Under the first heading Reid gives the example of a general purpose of studying law. To aim at studying law is not to regulate your conduct by a rule—there may be nothing of substance in common between the train of actions that one future lawyer follows and that of another, for instance, other than the fact that they both tend toward the same end—but it is to perform conduct that instantiates a pattern. The pattern in this case is constituted by an end; the actions in the train all tend towards the same end and interlock in such a way as to serve that end (relative, perhaps, to the agent's beliefs). Under the second heading—that is, general purposes of acting in accordance with some rule—fall all those cases of aiming to bring about a *codifiable* pattern of conduct, a pattern of events, that is, in which the pattern can be captured by a set of rules that the events in the train instantiate. It is in this category that Reid places character traits.

He gives the example of justice, saying that it is "a fixed purpose, or determination, to act according to the rules of justice, when there is opportunity" (*EAP* II. 3, p. 85/540*a*). Reid goes on to say that, "What has been said of justice, may be so easily applied to every other moral virtue, that it is unnecessary to give instances. They are all fixed purposes of acting according to a certain rule" (*EAP* II. 3, p. 85/540*a*). So, by extension, the trait of wisdom is a fixed purpose to act according to the rules of wisdom, when there is opportunity. Although character traits are the only examples that Reid gives here of general purposes of acting according to certain rules, there is one important difference between those to which he is referring here and other general purposes of acting according to rules. Those to which he is referring here are "fixed" purposes; they involve a "determination" to act according to a certain rule. Reid describes such fixed purposes as being instances of "virtues". The virtuous resolve to act in accordance with the right rules, and act in accordance with them with almost no exception. Most of us are not much like this, as Reid is well aware (cf. *EAP* II. 4, pp. 93/542*b*–543*b*). What is the difference between the virtuous and those who fall short of virtue? We might think that the difference lies in the degree to which our purposes, as opposed to those of the virtuous, are fixed. That is, we might think that we are less than fixed in our resolutions, while the virtuous resolutely act in accord with the rules of virtue. However, this is not Reid's view. He writes:

A man who has no general fixed purposes, may be said, as Pope says of most women, I hope unjustly, to have no character at all. He will be honest or dishonest, benevolent or malicious, compassionate or cruel, as the tide of his passions and affections drives him. This, however, I believe, is the case of but a few in advanced life, and these, with regard to conduct, the weakest and most contemptible of the species. (*EAP* II. 3, p. 88/541b)

Reid holds then that each of us, as far as we are from virtue, adheres, for the most part, to our fixed purposes; we obey the rules that we have established for ourselves. We have characters, they are just less than perfect. What follows is that where we differ from one another, and from the virtuous, is not in the degree to which we are fixedly committed to the rules by which we act, but, instead *in the rules to which we are fixedly committed*. Someone might, for instance, fall short of honesty because the rule by which he guides his conduct is "don't lie for profit unless you're in a hurry". This is a rule to which he is fixedly committed, it just isn't the rule to which the virtuous person is committed. The claim is that for every character trait, even those that fall short of virtues, there is a corresponding rule to which an agent possessing that character trait is fixedly committed.

So, for Reid, there are two features of an agent that make it the case that he has some particular character trait: his conduct follows a codifiable, rule-based pattern, and it follows that pattern because he has committed himself to following such a pattern. Reid is insistent that this second condition is required; the first is not sufficient. Commenting on his account of character traits, he writes,

By this, the virtues may be easily distinguished, in thought at least, from natural affections that bear the same name. Thus, benevolence is a capital virtue, which, though not so necessary to the being of society, is entitled to a higher degree of approbation than even justice. But there is a natural affection of benevolence common to good and bad men, to the virtuous and to the vicious. How shall these be distinguished?

In practice, indeed, we cannot distinguish them in other men, and with difficulty in ourselves; but in theory, nothing is more easy. The virtue of benevolence is a fixed purpose or resolution to do good when we have opportunity, from a conviction that it is right, and is our duty. The affection of benevolence is a propensity to do good, from natural constitution or habit, without regard to rectitude or duty. (*EAP* II. 3, pp. 85–86/540b)

So, imagine two agents who lead parallel lives, each performing just the same actions from just the same desires, sentiments, or affections, at just the same times. If one of the agents has a fixed resolution to act in accord with the rule of benevolence, that agent is benevolent. The agent who simply has benevolent desires at all the right times, but never resolves to act benevolently, is not. The first has the virtue of benevolence, the second merely a benevolent temperament.[8] Notice that neither of these agents experiences any struggle. Both act just as their sentiments direct, and so neither feels the pain that comes with action contrary to one's affective leanings. We could put the difference between the agent with the virtue of benevolence and the agent with the benevolent temperament like this. Both act according to a rule. The person with the virtue of benevolence acts according to the rule "Help others according to their due, whenever there is opportunity." The person with the benevolent temperament acts according to the rule "Act as dictated by one's sentiments." As it happens, these two rules specify precisely the same actions to the two agents because the second agent has sentiments that favor just those actions that accord with the rule of benevolence. But this is a lucky accident: were the second agent's sentiments to be different, his actions would diverge from those of the first agent. What this implies is that they differ only counter-factually. The agent with the virtue of benevolence would act benevolently even if he had, counter to fact, contrary inclinations; the agent with the benevolent temperament, on the other hand, would not act benevolently if his sentiments inclined him differently.

Why does Reid think that the person with the benevolent temperament lacks a trait of character, rather than thinking that that person has a trait of character—selfishness—which just happens to differ from the trait of character of the benevolent person? Why not say, that is, that the person with the benevolent temperament is fixedly committed to the rule "Do as my sentiments direct", where the truly benevolent person is fixedly committed to the rule "Do the benevolent thing"? If this were the right thing to say, then the person with the benevolent temperament would have a trait of character, contrary to what Reid holds. The answer would seem to come from the notion of "fixed commitment". That is, Reid, it seems, would claim that the person with the benevolent temperament is not fixedly committed to the rule "Do as my sentiments direct" although it is true that his conduct conforms to this rule. To see why he would think this, we need a better grip on the notion of "fixed commitment".

To be fixedly committed to a rule is not simply for one's conduct to conform to the rule. It is, also, to take the following of that rule as one's reason

---

[8] The distinction being drawn here is directly parallel to Kant's distinction between the agent who merely acts in accord with the moral law and the agent who acts from the moral law (cf. Immanuel Kant, "Groundwork of the Metaphysics of Morals", in *Practical Philosophy: The Cambridge Edition of the Works of Immanuel Kant*, tr. and ed. M. J. Gregor (Cambridge: Cambridge University Press, 1996), 61).

for following it. One who is fixedly committed to a rule follows that rule *so that* his conduct will conform to it.[9] This is the import of saying that character traits are an example of general purposes: one who has a general purpose sees the point of acting as being the instantiation of a pattern of conduct. Someone who reliably acts as directed by his sentiments may not be fixedly committed to the rule "Do as my sentiments direct", because such a person may never take the fact that his sentiments direct him to do something as his reason for doing it. His reason for feeding the child might be that he can't stand to see him suffer; he needn't ever guide himself by a conception of the act as conforming to either the selfish rule or the benevolent one, even though he ends up obeying both. So, Reid would say that someone who is fixedly committed to the rule "Do as my sentiments direct" does have a trait of character: he's selfish. However, the person with the benevolent temperament does not have even that character trait because his conduct does not express a fixed commitment to either that rule or the rule of benevolence; it does not express the fact that the person is guiding his behavior in accordance with a conception of the rule under which it falls.

Thus, in between the person with the benevolent temperament who has no character at all, and the person with the trait of benevolence, lies a third sort of agent: someone who has the trait associated with the rule "Do as my sentiments direct". Such a person does have a character trait, but it is not the trait of benevolence. He differs from the person with the benevolent temperament by virtue of the fact that he, and not the agent with the benevolent temperament, is fixedly committed to the rule that both agents obey; he differs from the virtuous person by virtue of the difference in the rules to which each is fixedly committed.[10]

The difference between the benevolent person and the person with the benevolent temperament can help us to identify another condition on the possession of a fixed purpose of acting in accordance with a rule of

[9] Notice that this makes sense of Reid's suggestion, in the passage just quoted, that a benevolent person does benevolent things because it is his duty to do so. Someone who takes the following of the rule of benevolence to be his reason for following it thereby takes the fact that he instantiates benevolence in his conduct, and thereby does his duty, as his reason for doing the benevolent thing.

[10] Because fixed commitment to a rule requires guidance of one's conduct by a conception of the rule under which one's conduct falls, a train or sequence of actions is a far better indicator of the fact that an agent has a particular character trait than any single action could be. It seems much more likely that an agent who performs multiple actions that fall into a pattern is aiming to instantiate that pattern in his conduct than an agent who performs only one such act.

conduct: if a person has such a fixed purpose, then he will behave in accordance with the rule to which he is fixedly committed across a wide range of circumstances, and particularly across changes in his passing sentiments; his conduct, that is, is stable under alterations in his sentiments. As Reid puts the point:

In men who have no fixed rules of conduct, no self-government, the natural temper is variable by numberless accidents. The man who is full of affection and benevolence this hour, when a cross accident happens to ruffle him, or perhaps when an easterly wind blows, feels a strange revolution in his temper. The kind and benevolent affections give place to the jealous and malignant, which are as readily indulged in their turn, and for the same reason, because he feels a propensity to indulge them. (*EAP* II. 3, p. 86/540b; see also *EAP* III. 2.viii, pp. 197–8/578b)

The actions of an agent who has a benevolent temperament are not indicative of the presence in the world of a reliable source of benevolent actions. He acts on whatever sentiments happen to be ascendant in his psyche, and nothing assures that his benevolent sentiments will always be the ascendant; they may change "when an easterly wind blows". When an agent possesses a character trait, on the other hand, his actions occur in accordance with a rule *because* the agent sees to it that he acts in accordance with that rule no matter what sentiments nature happens to spring on him. The ordering of his actions is non-accidental, not left to happenstance to produce.

The conformity to the rule of the conduct of the agent who has a character trait, then, is counterfactually stable. But how stable does the agent's conformity need to be to justify the claim that the agent has a *fixed* purpose? At one extreme is conduct that necessarily conforms to the rule in question: in every like circumstance across possible worlds, the agent acts in a like manner. At the other extreme is conduct that is not at all modally stable: there is no saying how the agent acts in like circumstances in non-actual possible worlds. How stably need the agent be dedicated to a rule of conduct to justify the claim to be fixed in his purpose to act in accordance with the rule? Although Reid says little about the matter, it is possible that Reid thinks of the behavior of an agent with a character trait to be just stable enough to justify inferences to the effect that he will follow the relevant rule in similar circumstances in the future. He writes:

It may surely be expected, that of the various actions within the sphere of [free agents's] power, they will choose what pleases them most for the present, or what appears to be most for their real, though distant good. When there is a competition between these motives, the foolish will prefer present gratification; the wise, the greater and more distant good. (*EAP* IV. 4, pp. 291–2/612*b*)

Without knowing whether the agent is foolish or wise, we know only that he will do either the foolish thing or the wise thing, but we can't determine which. But given the extra piece of information about his character, we can infer what he will do. The inference in such a case, however, is not a deductive inference. In the preceding paragraph, Reid puts the point like this: "[W]e reason from men's motives to their actions, and, in many cases, with great probability, but never with absolute certainty" (EAP IV. 4, p. 291/612*a*). The distinction between probable inferences and inferences that yield certain conclusions is the distinction between inductive and deductive inferences. This suggests that, for Reid, we have as good reason to legitimately expect the benevolent person to do the benevolent thing as we have to expect the unsupported object to fall; we have a guarantee of the same strength as the guarantee that we have that nature will be uniform. As Hume has shown (Reid thinks), it is perfectly possible that such expectations will be disappointed: it is logically possible that the next unsupported object will not fall, and it is logically possible that the benevolent person will fail to do the benevolent thing at his next opportunity. But, nonetheless, very often expectations of uniformity are both justified and rewarded. Character, in short, provides the grounding for expectations of conduct that accords with the rule corresponding to the character trait in question.

It is not easy to determine the degree of stability of conformity to a rule that is necessary to justify an inference to the effect that the agent will conform to the rule. For instance, imagine someone who self-consciously makes an effort to conform his conduct to the rule "Protect others from harm, when there is opportunity", and would do what's necessary to do so across a wide variety of circumstances, including circumstances in which he really doesn't feel like doing what's required to obey the rule. Nonetheless, this person could be actually guided by the rule "Protect my family from harm, when there is opportunity", although he happens to live in isolation from everyone other than his family. (He might even recognize this fact about himself were he to direct his attention to his true motives.[11]) Such a person does not have the character trait associated with the rule "Protect others from harm, when there is opportunity"—he is not

---

[11] See Ch. 1 for discussion of the sense, for Reid, in which we are and are not aware of our own motives.

fixedly committed to that rule—despite the fact that his conduct can be legitimately expected to conform to that rule in a wide variety of circumstances, and he has it as his aim to conform his conduct to the rule. The reason he is not fixedly committed to the rule specifying protection even of strangers is that he would not follow that rule in some circumstances that he may never face: he would not do so, for instance, if protecting a stranger from harm would require not protecting one of his family members from harm. Thus, it would not be legitimate to infer that this person would follow the rule "Protect others from harm, when there is opportunity" in certain hypothetical circumstances. Of course, we have a similar problem with respect to any regularity in nature: there is always the possibility that the law that we identify simply happens by chance to align with the actual laws guiding the progress of nature. So whatever degree of certainty we can have in any inductive inference is the degree of certainty we can have that the person with a character trait will obey the rule under which we subsume his conduct.

Reid explicitly draws the connection between human character traits and the source of regularity in the natural world. He writes: "A law of nature is a purpose or resolution of the author of nature, to act according to a certain rule—either immediately by himself, or by instruments that are under his direction" (*COR* 93, p. 176). Wherever there is a regularity, for Reid, there is a corresponding trait of character, for there is a corresponding fixed purpose to act as dictated by the relevant rule. A regularity in human conduct springs from a human trait of character; a regularity in nature from a trait of character of God. To have a trait of character, for Reid, is to be self-consciously rule-governed in one's efforts with sufficient fixity to provide as much justification for inferences about how one will act as can be had for inductive inferences.

We can summarize the results of this section, then, as follows:

> *Reidian Character Traits*: An agent is fixedly committed to a particular rule of conduct *if and only if* (1) he has it as his aim to conform his conduct to that rule, and (2) inferences to the effect that he will act according to the rule are as legitimate as any justified inductive inference.

Premise (4.1): From End-Directedness to Wisdom

So, a wise person is someone who is fixedly committed to "the rules of wisdom". Given the definition developed in the previous section of "fixed commitment to a rule", it follows that, where there is wise conduct, there is end-directed conduct; the end in question is that of acting according to the rules of wisdom. But why should we think that where there is end-directed conduct there is necessarily wise conduct, as premise (4.1) claims? After all, where there is benevolent conduct, there is also end-directed conduct. Why should it follow that where there is benevolent conduct there is wise conduct? That is, it doesn't appear that end-directed events need to follow "the rules of wisdom". They could instantiate entirely different rules. Further, recall Reid's distinction between the different sorts of general purposes: those that involve a commitment to a general rule, and those that involve commitment to a general end. The conduct in which one engages when one is committed to a general end (or a particular end, for that matter) are, indeed, end-directed events, but they don't seem to instantiate any rule, much less "the rules of wisdom". So, there is at least one reason to doubt that end-directedness presupposes wisdom: end-directed conduct doesn't seem necessarily to be aimed at instantiating the rules of wisdom.

There is another reason to think that end-directedness does not presuppose wisdom. Even if in aiming at an end one is, *ipso facto*, aiming to instantiate the rules of wisdom, one might not be fixedly committed to those rules. It seems possible to be aiming to obey the rules of wisdom and, still, for inferences to the conclusion that one will act as dictated by those rules to be ungrounded. After all, knowing that a person is trying to do something, does not, all by itself, justify one in thinking that the person will do it: he might not have either the capacity or the power to do it. We could know that a person was trying to be wise or good and still not think him wise or good, for to try is not to succeed. To overcome these difficulties, and thus to establish that end-directedness does indeed presuppose wisdom, we need to understand better how exactly Reid thinks of wisdom.

Reid gives only hints as to exactly how he understands the character trait of wisdom; that is, he gives little more than hints as to what he takes the rules of wisdom to be. He does, however, seem to equate wisdom with prudence, writing in his statement of the third argument for moral liberty,

It is of no consequence in this argument, whether one has made the best choice of his main end or not; whether his end be riches, or power, or fame, or the approbation of his Maker. I suppose only that he has prudently and steadily pursued it; that, in a long course of deliberate actions, he has taken the means most conducive to his end, and avoided whatever might cross it.

That such conduct in a man demonstrates a certain degree of wisdom and understanding, no man ever doubted. (*EAP*, IV. 8, p. 321/622*b*)

Elsewhere he writes,

We account him a wise man who is wise for himself; and, if he prosecutes this end through difficulties and temptations that lie in his way, his character is far superior to that of the man who, having the same end in view, is continually starting out of the road to it, from an attachment to his appetites and passions, and doing every day what he knows he shall heartily repent. (*EAP* III. 3. iv, p. 218/585*a*)

Reid seems to think of the wise person as someone who has ends, recognizes how to achieve them, and is not distracted from his purpose. We might think of the wise person as the connoisseur of end-directedness. The wise person can appreciate all of the relations that any particular event bears to his ends. He recognizes that a particular event is likely to lead to his end, and is an efficient or inefficient way to get there, and depends for its effectiveness as a means on the occurrence of various other events whose relation to his ends he also appreciates. Of course, appreciation isn't enough for wisdom: the wise person also makes every effort to bring about those events that exhibit all the end-related virtues to the highest degree.

An end-directed event is brought about because of the relation that it bears to the end in question. An event is not end-directed just because it serves the end; it must also be brought about for the sake of serving the end. So every end-directed event is brought about because it instantiates a particular relation to the end that is appreciated by the wise person. If to be guided by the rules of wisdom is to be guided by an appreciation of the relations that various events bear to one's ends, then all end-directed events are, indeed, in conformity *to some degree* with the rules of wisdom. An example might be useful: imagine that I can light a candle by striking a match or by focusing sunlight through a magnifying glass. The former option is the better choice: it requires less effort and is faster, and I'm lazy and in a hurry. Still, I don't appreciate that and use the magnifying glass instead. If the events of my focusing the sunlight through the magnifying glass are end-directed, then I must appreciate the positive relation that those events bear to the end of lighting the candle; they will lead to that result, and I can see that. If I didn't appreciate that, then those events couldn't be said to be directed towards the end of lighting the candle. True, I don't appreciate the comparative weakness of using the magnifying glass rather than a match, but, still, I do appreciate part of what a perfectly wise person would appreciate fully. So although my conduct does not fall under the perfect rules of wisdom, it falls under rules that are close to the rules of wisdom. My conduct falls under a rule that corresponds to a character trait that might be described as "imperfect wisdom". And so because of the particular nature of wisdom, there is reason to think that all end-directed events are, by their nature, in conformity with the rules of *some degree* of wisdom.

It still remains to be shown that end-directed events provide for the possibility of justified inferences to the conclusion that similar events will occur in similar circumstances. If end-directed events are to be indicative of wisdom, that is, it is not enough that there is an effort to conform to the rules of wisdom; there must also be a resolution to engage in that effort that is sufficiently strong to ground an inference that has as much justification as an inductive inference. It might seem that Reid cannot allow that *all* end-directed events can be justifiably expected in similar circumstances since he allows for the possibility of end-directed events that serve particular purposes, rather than general purposes (cf. *EAP* II. 3, p. 84/539b). By their nature, particular purposes do not involve a commitment to similar events in similar circumstances: to have such a commitment is to have a purpose that is served through the performance of any one of a number of possible particular events all of which have something or other in common. But then one's purpose is general, not particular. So, if an end-directed event is end-directed by virtue of its relation to a particular purpose, it would appear that the end-directed event is not indicative of the sort of quality required to ground an inference to the conclusion that a similar event will occur in similar circumstances.

Notice that the issue here is very similar to that involved in discussions of one-time, or first-time, causation, often raised in connection with Hume's account of the causal relation. Hume is sometimes charged with an inability to account for the fact that one event can be the cause of another even when there is no history—and perhaps no future—in which events similar to the first are followed by events similar to the second. This problem could be posed as one about justified inductive inference: couldn't the world be sufficiently stable to allow us justifiably to expect a particular event to follow one we have observed even though there is no history of conjunction of the two types of events? If so, then the fact that events can be end-directed by virtue of their relation to particular purposes does not, in itself, invalidate the claim that the end-directedness of an event justifies an expectation of similar events in the future.

In fact, Reid was probably the first person to criticize Hume's view of causation on the grounds of its inability to account for one-time causation. He writes that, under Hume's account of causation, "whatever was singular in its nature, or the first thing of its kind, could have no cause" (*EAP* IV. 9, p. 335/627b; see also *COR* 123, p. 234), and he clearly takes this to speak against Hume's account. Thus, so long as we allow that the links between events needed to support inductive inferences could be in place even where there is no history of law-like behavior, there is no obstacle to thinking that events similar to those that are end-directed by virtue of their relation to particular purposes can be justifiably expected to occur in similar circumstances.

But to remove an apparent obstacle to the acceptance of a claim is not to provide a reason to accept it. It is undeniable that an event can be end-directed even if its agent is not decided upon doing things similar in every respect in circumstances similar in every respect. I might decide to have a second drink at dinner this one time—and the events involved would be end-directed on the grounds that they were decided upon—and I might leave it at that, and never have a second drink with similar dinners in similar situations in the future. No one could be in position to infer justifiably that I will take a second drink with dinner tomorrow based on my behavior today, even if tomorrow is similar to today in all the relevant respects. However, in taking the second drink, I am also acting on a general purpose: a general purpose of doing wise things, or things that bear some appropriate relation to my ends. If this were not so, the taking of the second drink would not be end-directed at all. So, it might be said in Reid's defense that every end-directed event does involve a general purpose of doing end-directed things, and so a person who acts in an end-directed way can be expected to act in an end-directed way in the future. There need not be much uniformity in an agent's conduct for this to be the case: he might take a second drink today and only one tomorrow and still be acting, on both occasions, with end-directedness itself as part of his goal.

This section began with two problems for premise (4.1). First, it seemed possible for events to be end-directed and yet aimed at instantiating patterns very different from the pattern distinctive of wisdom, or aimed at instantiating no patterns at all; second, it seemed possible for events to be aimed without providing the grounds for expectations of future similar events in future similar circumstances. Both problems are solved by recognizing the special qualities of wisdom: to be wise is to be fixedly committed to acting from an appreciation of the relations between possible events and one's ends. But for an event to be end-directed, it must spring from an appreciation of the relations that it bears to an agent's ends. End-directedness is the byproduct of wisdom, and can only be achieved through wisdom's exercise.

Premise (4.2): From Wisdom to Power

Premise (4.2) seems, at first glance, to be false. Why can't wisdom be expressed by an effect, or series of effects, even when the wise agent is not the efficient cause of the effect or effects? For instance, say that I form a detailed and brilliant plan about how to rob the British Museum. Thinking of it as only an idle exercise, I drop my notes in a trashcan where they are picked up by some idiotic thieves, capable of executing, but incapable of planning a robbery of the sort described. Imagine that they follow my instructions to the letter and successfully rob the museum. I did not have the power to make them rob the museum and exert that power; they did what they did on their own, and so I am not the efficient cause of their conduct. Still, I might take pride in the robbery when I read about it in the paper the next day; I might be proud, that is, that I was shrewd enough to rob the museum, even if I didn't do it myself. But if the feeling of pride is justified in this case, then their conduct would appear to be expressive of my wisdom, even though I am not the efficient cause of their conduct.[12]

---

[12] This example is not a flat counterexample to the claim that "Every indication of wisdom, taken from the effect, is equally an indication of power to execute what wisdom planned." Reid intends that claim only to apply to cases in which "the effect" consists of actions performed by the same agent whose wisdom they express. This is not the case in the example just described. However, the point that the example seems to illustrate is that it is not generally true that the features of a thing are only expressed by the thing's "effects" in Reid's strong sense of "effect". A creature's talent for planning robberies can be expressed even by features of the world that are not produced by the creature's exertion of his power to produce them. In fact, his wisdom, in this sense, can be expressed by an event even if he lacks the power to produce it. This leaves premise (4.2) without an adequate justification. In *Thomas Reid*, p. 277, Keith Lehrer brings up an objection to the third argument on something very close to these lines. Lehrer tries to respond on Reid's behalf by claiming that while the evidence of moral liberty on the part of the actors—in our case, the criminals who execute my plan to rob the museum—is not demonstratively decisive, it is good inductive evidence, and so shouldn't be disparaged. I don't believe that this is how Reid would respond to such examples. The remainder of my discussion will demonstrate this, but one small point is appropriate here: Reid explicitly says that the third argument is just as strong as Samuel Clarke's proof of God's existence (*EAP* IV. 8, pp. 324–5/623b–624a), and there is little doubt that Reid considers that argument to be a demonstration (cf. *EAP* IV. 9, p. 338/628b). Since inductive arguments of the sort Lehrer has in mind are not demonstrations, Reid must not take the third argument to be inductive.

Reid would not be troubled by this example, because under his conception of character traits, the thieves' conduct is not expressive of my wisdom. The execution of my plan might be expressive of various good (or bad) things about me, but if I didn't efficiently cause the conduct, then it is not expressive of a fixed resolution to follow the rules of wisdom, for inferences about what I will do when faced with the opportunity to do a wise thing are not justified; from the fact that the thieves did what I planned it cannot be inferred that either I, or the thieves, will do something wise in the future when given the opportunity. As was suggested in Chapter 3, to deny that a pattern of behavior indicates either that there is power or that there is a resolution to employ it in a consistent manner is to deny that we are justified in our reliance on the inductive principle. However, to assert that a train of behavior indicates a character trait of a particular creature is to assert that we can rely on the creature to act in like ways in like future circumstances. However, we cannot rely on the creature to act in accordance with the relevant rule solely on the strength of the fact that the creature makes every effort to conform its behavior to the rule: try as one might, without power one won't necessarily succeed in doing what one tries to do. Consistency in exertion by itself doesn't guarantee sameness of effect; power is also required. So, if we rely on a creature to conform its behavior to a principle of conduct, we must be relying on its possession of power. Thus, built into Reid's notion of a character trait is the notion of power.

Reid expresses almost precisely this point in the following passage:

> Every man who pursues an end, be it good or bad, must be active when he is disposed to be indolent; he must rein every passion and appetite that would lead him out of his road.
>
> Mortification and self-denial are found not in the paths of virtue only; they are common to every road that leads to an end, be it ambition, or avarice, or even pleasure itself. Every man who maintains an uniform and consistent character, must sweat and toil, and often struggle with his present inclination. (*EAP* III. 2. viii, p. 198/579a)

Reid's point here is that to be end-directed in the manner in which someone who possesses a character trait is end-directed, requires the capacity to act contrary to the "passion[s] and appetite[s]" with which such a person finds himself, and which point him away from his end. If we take seriously the idea that such a person does not pursue his end—does not, for instance, conform his conduct to the rule of wisdom—solely by virtue of the lucky possession of some other motive, such as a motive that favors wise actions, then we must think that his conduct conforms to the rule because the person possesses some capacity that goes beyond the capacity to be moved by his inclinations. This is to ascribe such a person with the power to pursue his end, and with a resolution to exert that power consistently. It is because character involves consistency of conduct even in the face of competing inclinations that it also involves active power and a resolution to exert it consistently.

In short, then, I suggest the following argument in support of premise (4.2):

(4.2i) If a sequence of actions indicates that S is wise, then the sequence indicates that S aims at obeying the rule of wisdom, and we are justified in expecting S to do the wise thing.

(4.2ii) If S aims at obeying the rule of wisdom, but either lacks the power to obey it or the resolution to exercise that power in conformity with it, then we are not justified in expecting S to do the wise thing.

∴ If a sequence of actions indicates that S is wise, then it indicates that S is the efficient cause of each of the actions in the sequence. (Premise (4.2))[13]

The work of this argument—and thus of the third argument for moral liberty—is done by two things: by the account of character, and by the claim that where there is a justified inductive inference there is power and a tendency to exert it in a consistent manner. As was suggested briefly in Chapter 3, the second of these two claims is far from obvious. It simply isn't clear that more in the way of justification of inductive inferences is provided by appeal to power and a resolution to exert it consistently than is done by flat appeal to stable regularities that are not grounded in any

---

[13] I presented this way of reading the third argument from moral liberty at a conference in 2000 where Paul Hoffman served as my commentator. Hoffman objected to my reading of the argument, writing, "On Yaffe's reconstruction, the argument hinges on a positive account of wisdom, that it is a fixed resolution. But it seems to me that Reid's argument in fact depends on a negative account of wisdom, namely, that wisdom by itself cannot execute." (This quotation was used with Hoffman's permission.) Notice, however, that if Reid's only point is that a wise being cannot, on those grounds alone, bring anything about, then the conclusion that he is interested in establishing (namely that human beings have moral liberty), would not follow from his premises. Even if we were to grant that wisdom alone is not enough to bring about a wise act, we might conclude that human beings, wise as they are, are not the efficient causes of their actions. We might think those actions caused by God, or we might deny them to be efficiently caused at all. Only if there is some reason to believe wisdom to require power does the argument have any force.

metaphysical facts of this sort. However, more can be said, and needs to be said, about Reid's account of character. If there is something about character traits that supports the thought that an agent who has one must be resolved, in the requisite sense, to exert his power in a consistent manner, then the argument behind Reid's acceptance of the claim that where there's wisdom there's power may rest on more than it appears; it appears to rest on the assertion of a metaphysics that somehow provides for the justification of our inferences, but in some way that eludes specification. Yet perhaps there is something in our ordinary conception of character traits that supports Reid's argument. Perhaps, that is, when we ascribe a person with a character trait we ordinarily take ourselves to be saying that he is endowed with power and resolved to exert it consistently.

But is this so? Is there anything about our character attributions that supports this claim? It is important to be clear that the belief that an agent with a character trait will exert himself in a similar manner in similar circumstances—that he will, in fact, make an effort to act according to the rule associated with the relevant trait of character—is not enough to support Reid's third argument for moral liberty. If the argument is to succeed, in ascribing a character trait to a person we must believe that there is something about the person, something that lies beyond our capacity to explain or give reasons, that accounts for the regularity of his exertions of power. We must believe, that is, that he is resolved to exert his power in a consistent manner in just the way in which, Reid thinks, God must be resolved to exert his powers if we are to be justified in making the assumption that the future will be like the past. But what reason is there for thinking that our character attributions are guided by this assumption?

Reid seems to equate morally responsible conduct with conduct that is reflective of character. And he seems to equate morally responsible conduct with conduct for which the agent is accountable, or, more literally, of which the agent must be in position to offer an account; an agent is morally responsible for a bit of behavior if and only if it is appropriate for the authority that imposes the standards with respect to which the agent is to be assessed to demand an explanation from the agent for his behavior (cf. *EIP* VI. 5, pp. 478–9). Such an explanation might first subsume the agent's behavior under a law; in explaining his behavior, that is, the agent might identify a rule with which he aimed to comply and under which his conduct falls. The agent can then be asked appropriately why he acted in accordance with this law. The agent might, at this point, cite a more general law under which his conduct falls until, ultimately, he reaches a law that is basic—a law, that is, with which he complies for its own sake, and not because by obeying it he obeys a more general law. Reid's thought is that if the agent is to be held responsible for his behavior, then there must be an answer to the question why he acted in accordance with this most basic law. The answer will not amount to giving the agent's reason for obeying the basic law: if the agent has such a reason, the law would not be basic; if the agent had some reason for conforming his behavior to the law, then he would not guide his conduct in accordance with it for its own sake. (This would be so, even if his reason were that it is his duty to do so. By citing such a reason, he identifies a more basic law—"Do my duty"—to which his behavior conforms.) Instead, the answer to the question "Why does he act in accordance with the basic law governing his behavior?" will simply be that the agent is resolved to exert himself so as to comply with the basic law. To cite this resolution is to cite that fact about the agent by virtue of which he obeys the basic law under which his conduct falls without citing anything that makes it intelligible, or reasonable, why he should so act. It is not to give a further reason that the agent accepts and that guides his behavior, but, instead, to gesture to the existence of some fact about the agent's nature, a fact the citing of which provides no further degree of intelligibility to his conduct.

Is there reason to think that our ordinary character attributions presuppose this sort of structure? It is undeniable that we think of character attributions as identifying deeper facts about persons than merely the laws with respect to which they act. Asserting that an agent is selfish or benevolent is doing something quite different from identifying the laws that govern, say, his digestion. We think of our character attributions as capturing something about agents that goes beyond regularity in behavior. This is why it is possible to say of an agent who has done nothing but lie that he is not, in fact, a liar. Such a claim would make no sense if to call an agent a liar was simply to say that he lies. A person is a liar not just because he lies but also because it is part of his nature to lie. What does this mean? What more is asserted in saying it is in the agent's nature than was asserted in saying that he lies? When we make such claims we are gesturing towards the stable and enduring feature of the agent in virtue of which he lies, a feature that resides beyond the horizon of observable behavior. We think, that is, that we are identifying something like a resolution to exert his power in a consistent manner, to aim himself towards lying. If this is right, then in so far as ordinary character attributions are conceived of as ultimate—as capturing features of the agent's fundamental moral nature—they proceed from a presumption of power and resolution to exert it consistently. In our ordinary character attributions, that is, we take ourselves to be identifying features of agents that transcend the regularities under which they act and provide the grounds for the persistence of patterns in their behavior.

Conclusion

In Chapter 3, an effort was made to understand Reid's appeal to the presence of power and the resolution to exert it consistently as part of his effort to point to those features of the universe by virtue of which it marches on with sufficient regularity to ground our expectations of its regularity. It's not just that things will be as they were; something assures that it will be so. We can call that something "power and the resolution to exert it consistently", but in doing so we make no progress towards understanding how this something makes it the case that our inductive inferences are justified; the metaphysics does the work but there is no hope of understanding the mechanisms by virtue of which it does it, or even of believing that the term "mechanism" is apt for identifying the relation between the metaphysics and the regularity we encounter. Still, it was suggested, given Reid's providentialist perspective—his view that all events are end-directed—he is in position to argue that behind all change there is power and the necessary resolution, if he can show that the very idea of end-directedness requires power and such a resolution. It was that task that was taken up in this chapter.

What has emerged is that the link between end-directedness and power is ultimately rooted in Reid's account of one of the central concepts, not of metaphysics, but of moral philosophy: the concept of character. For Reid, the relation between character and regularities in behavior is the same as the relation between, on the one hand, power and the resolution to exert it consistently, and, on the other, regularity in nature. Both regularities have their basis in facts that lie beyond intelligibility and that we have the right to believe in only because our ordinary practices presuppose them. In relying on nature to be regular we must believe that something assures its regularity; in taking others to be honest, cruel, benevolent, and selfish we must believe that something in their natures assures that they will be so. In neither case is the grounds of our belief a rational one: we recognize neither a deductive nor inductive link between the something and the observable facts. But nonetheless we are committed to the presence of these somethings; we are committed, that is, to thinking that in the universe, and in others, lie powers and the resolution to exert them with regularity.

5

The Influence of Motives: The Push of Power?

Any adequate theory of action must accommodate the obvious and undeniable fact that acts are motivated; we act for reasons. If the influence of motives on action were a species of causal influence, then there would be good reason to reject Reid's equation between an agent's actions and those events of which the agent is the efficient cause. After all, if a person's behavior is produced by power that flows either from or through his motives, power that does not belong to the person whose behavior it is, then it is possible for a person to engage in motivated behavior of which he is not the efficient cause. However, motivated behavior is end-directed behavior, and so to assert that motivational influence is causal influence, and thereby imply that motivated behavior is not efficiently caused by the agent whose behavior it is, would be to break the link between end-directedness and power discussed in Chapter 4. Therefore, a full defense of Reid's theory of action requires rejection of a pair of claims: that motives are the efficient causes of behavior, and that motives are the physical causes of behavior. This chapter is concerned with Reid's argument against the former of these claims; the next with the latter.

Given that Reid holds that all efficient causes have will and understanding, and so must have minds, showing that motives are not efficient causes would seem to be an easy task: they don't think, so they aren't efficient causes. However, Reid does not offer this as his reason for denying that motives are efficient causes, nor does he think that claim easy to show. He writes,

Suppose, now, that you take the word cause in the strict sense [that is, in the sense of efficient causation]; its relation to its effect is so self-evidently different from the relation of a motive to an action, that I am jealous of a mathematical demonstration of a truth so self-evident. Nothing is more difficult than to demonstrate what is self-evident.   (*COR* 93, p. 175)

As difficult as it is, however, in the very next breath Reid offers what appears to be an attempt, at least, to demonstrate the claim:

A cause is a being which has a real existence; a *motive* has no real existence, and, therefore, can have no active power. It is a thing conceived, and not a thing that exists; and, therefore, can neither be active nor even passive. To say that a motive really acts, is as absurd as to say that a motive drinks my health, or that a motive gives me a box on the ear.   (*COR* 93, p. 175; see also *EAP* IV. 4, pp. 283/608*b*–609*a*)

If this is intended as an argument, it is clear that its crucial premise is the claim that a motive is "a thing conceived, and not a thing that exists". However, this premise faces some obvious difficulties. First, it is not clear that any work is done in establishing the argument's conclusion by the claim that a motive is "a thing conceived": if motives don't exist, and all efficient causes do, then motives aren't efficient causes whether or not they are "things conceived". Further, it seems patently false to say that motives don't exist. Understood as thoughts about possible actions, motives exist in whatever sense any other thoughts exist; they are modifications of mind. Understood as the objects of thoughts—as what a thought is of, or about— they often exist; we are often motivated, that is, by actual features of our past, present, or future.

These two problems should be understood not as objections to Reid's argument for the claim that motives are not efficient causes, but, instead, as challenges for the interpreter of the argument. That is, any charitable interpretation of Reid's account of motives—his account of what motives are—is constrained in at least two ways: first, under the interpretation, the claim that motives are things conceived must be essential for establishing that they are not efficient causes; and, second, under the interpretation, the claim that motives do not exist, if not clearly true, can be understood in such a way that it is at least plausible. The aim of this chapter, then, is to make sense adequately of Reid's claim that motives are conceived but non-existent and to thereby expose the structure of Reid's brief argument for the claim that motives are not efficient causes of the behavior they motivate.

It should be noted that there is a clear and important historical precedent for the argument that Reid offers against the claim that motives are efficient causes of behavior. In his remarks on Anthony Collins's Necessitarian treatise *A Philosophical Enquiry Concerning Human Liberty*, Samuel Clarke writes: "[I]f it be said, that *Reasons* or *Motives* are the *Causes* of Action; this can be true only in a *figurative* Sense: For, to make *Reasons* or *Motives* the *literal* and *physical* Cause of Motion or Action, is supposing *abstract Notions* to be *Substances*" (*Works* iv. 728; see also pp. 725, 732). Clarke uses the term "physical cause" in precisely the opposite sense in which Reid uses it: he means what Reid means by "efficient cause". So, Clarke is claiming that motives are not efficient causes because they are not substances, and only substances are capable of being efficient causes. While Clarke does not claim that motives do not exist, he does claim, like Reid, that they belong in the wrong metaphysical category to be efficient causes. In fact, there is a deeper commonality between Clarke's argument and Reid's for Clarke claims that motives are "abstract notions", and Reid describes not only motives but fictional objects and universals as conceived but non-existent.[1] So, as will be shown in this chapter, the real force of both Reid's argument and Clarke's derives from the thought that motives for action are abstract objects of some sort. It is through reflection on what Reid has to say about non-existent objects of conception in general that we are able to get a grasp on his argument against the claim that motives are efficient causes, so that will be considered first.

Non-Existent Objects of Conception

As is well known, one of the great preoccupations of Reid's philosophical career was the refutation of "the theory of ideas" advocated, Reid holds, by Locke, Berkeley, and Hume.[2] As Reid understands the theory of ideas, every thought that has an object involves the perception of a mental entity, an idea, that exists in the mind of the perceiver. For our purposes here, the important thesis to which an advocate of the theory of ideas is committed, under Reid's view, is the claim that every thought has an *existent* object, including thoughts, such as thoughts about fictional objects, that also have non-existent objects. Reid thinks that the likes of Locke, Berkeley, and Hume are led to this view in part because they assume that in thinking

[1] He says also that a law of nature is "a thing conceived, and not a thing that exists" (*COR* 93, p. 175). Laws of nature, as we have seen in Ch. 3, are simply resolutions on God's part to act in a regular manner. That is, they are among God's motives. Hence the claim that laws of nature are conceived but not existent follows from the general claim about motives with which I am concerned here.

[2] In fact, Reid takes the theory of ideas to have been tacitly accepted by *all* his philosophical predecessors. See *EIP* II. 7 and II. 8.

there must be something that acts on the mind, or on which the mind acts; since things that don't exist can neither act nor be acted upon, it follows that in every thought there is some existent entity in the head, an idea, that acts on the mind or on which the mind acts. Reid, however, wishes to dissolve this motivation for the theory of ideas. With this aim, he writes, "If we can conceive objects which have no existence, it follows, that there may be objects of thought which neither act upon the mind, nor are acted upon by it; because that which has no existence can neither act nor be acted upon" (*EIP* IV. 2, p. 313). Reid's point here amounts to the same point, in different dress, that he makes in other contexts against the advocates of the theory of ideas: on what grounds are stricter requirements placed on the immediate perceptual relation than on the mediate? That is, why think that it is impossible immediately to perceive an object without either the object acting on the mind or the mind on the object, while holding that it is perfectly possible mediately to perceive an object with which the mind has no causal commerce? Without this asymmetry, the theory of ideas cannot hope to have solved the problem of the absence of causal connection between the mind and its object in thoughts about things that don't exist. After all, even if we agree that my mind might act on, or be acted upon, an *idea* of Pegasus, the existent and immediate object of thought, I'm still thinking about *Pegasus*, the mediate object of thought, something that does not exist, under the theory of ideas. If it's so important that the objects of thought exist, why not the mediate objects of thought? Without some explanation for the asymmetry in treatment of immediate and mediate objects of thought, the advocate of the theory of ideas cannot claim that ideas must be postulated in order to fill a causal gap between objects and the mind. What is of interest about this argument, for our purposes, is not its conclusion, but its central premise. Reid grants precisely the same status to non-existent objects of thought as he does to motives; and he draws the very same conclusion through reflection on their status: since they are conceived but non-existent, they cannot be efficient causes.

So, Reid has argued against one of the primary motivations for holding that in every thought about a thing there is some existent object of thought that is either identical to the thing or in some way closely related to it (as idea and object are supposed to be): one might be motivated to believe this on the grounds that thinking about a thing requires some kind of causal commerce between the mind and the thing; this is what Reid denies on the grounds that we think about non-existent things. But there is another possible motivation for the claim that every thought requires some existent object. We might hold this view because we think that thoughts fundamentally involve predication—to think about something is to ascribe a property to it—and predication requires two existent entities, corresponding to the subject and the predicate, one of which "adheres" in the other. Someone who holds this view might add that content-bearing entities (e.g. thoughts, sentences) are meaningful only if there is some entity that adheres in some other entity; the metaphysics, we might think, is what supplies content. Reid, however, denies that every thought involves predication; he thinks that a thought can have content, it can be about something, without predicating anything of that thing:

> Although there can be no judgment without a conception of the things about which we judge; yet conception may be without any judgment. Judgment can be expressed by a proposition only, and a proposition is a complete sentence; but simple apprehension may be expressed in a word or words, which make no complete sentence. (*EIP* VI. 1, p. 408)

To predicate we need to think about (in Reid's terminology "conceive of") a subject and predicate, and whatever other elements are required to create a complete sentence. But an individual thought about any one of those elements does not, itself, involve predication. Unless there are grounds for thinking that predication presupposes the existence of some subject and some predicate, over and above the claim that it requires thought about each of those elements, there is no reason to think that every thought about a thing has some existent object identical to or closely related to the thing.

To say that there need not be an existent object of every thought is not to say that there are, literally speaking, no objects of such thoughts. One might instead hold a position similar to that commonly attributed to Alexis Meinong according to which there is a mode of being different from that of full-fledged existence, but greater than true nothingness. One would then hold that in every thought about a thing there is some object of thought that has, at least, "being", if not existence; thoughts about Pegasus, then, would be thoughts about something that *is*, but does not exist. Some passages encourage the attribution of such a view to Reid. In discussing universals, which are the only things for which Reid thinks the term "idea" appropriate, he writes:

> [T]he whiteness of this sheet is one thing, whiteness is another; the conceptions signified by these two forms of speech are as different as the expressions: the first signifies an individual quality really existing, and is not a general conception, though it be an abstract one; the second signifies a general conception, which

implies no existence, but may be predicated of every thing that is white, and in the same sense.[3] On this account, if one should say, that the whiteness of this sheet is the whiteness of another sheet, every man perceives this to be absurd; but when he says both sheets are white, this is true and perfectly understood. The conception of whiteness implies no existence; it would remain the same, though every thing in the universe that is white were annihilated. (*EIP* V. 3, p. 367)

One might take Reid to be offering some form of Platonist position under which the universal, whiteness, has some Meinongian-style metaphysical status different from that of ordinary existent particulars, but also different from that of nothingness; how else are we to understand Reid's seemingly reifying talk of "whiteness"? In a recent paper, Ryan Nichols has argued persuasively that Reid's view should be understood differently.[4] Instead of allowing a mode of being that is more than nothing and less than existence, under Nichols's interpretation, Reid instead denies that an entity need have any positive degree of being in order to be thought of or predicated of. There are properties that universals, and any other non-existent objects of thought, have, on this view—including the property of being the objects of thought—and they simply don't need to be in order to have these properties, or, what's the same thing, in order to be truly predicated of. In support of this interpretation, consider the following remark:

[The Platonists] were led to give existence to ideas [that is, forms or universals], from the common prejudice, that every thing which is an object of conception must really exist; and having once given existence to ideas, the rest of their mysterious system about ideas followed of course. . . .

Take away the attribute of existence, and suppose them not to be things that exist, but things that are barely conceived, and all the mystery is removed; all that remains is level to the human understanding. (*EIP* V. 5, p. 386)

The final claim of this passage—that "all that remains is level to the human understanding"—is not consistent with the interpretation under which

---

[3] To have an "abstract" conception, for Reid, is to think about one of an object's qualities in isolation from the others with which it is conjoined; to have a general conception, by contrast, is to think about a universal (*EIP* V. 3, p. 365).
[4] Ryan Nichols, "Reid on Fictional Objects and the Way of Ideas", *Philosophical Quarterly*, 52/209 (Oct. 2002), 582–601. Nichols describes Reid's view as "Meinongian", but he understands Meinong's view differently from the way in which it is standardly understood. In this, he follows James Van Cleve's interpretation of Meinong. See James Van Cleve, "If Meinong is Wrong, is McTaggart Right?", *Philosophical Topics*, 24/1 (Spring 1996), 231–54. Another useful discussion of Reid's account of universals is Nicholas Wolterstorff, *Thomas Reid and the Story of Epistemology* (Cambridge: Cambridge University Press, 2001), 70–4.

Reid grants to non-existent objects of thought some degree of being greater than nothing, and yet less than existence; were there a tier on the metaphysical ladder above nothing, but below existence, then anything that occupies that tier would fail to be "level to the human understanding". But the claim is consistent with the view Nichols ascribes to Reid: universals are thought about, but simply don't exist, so there is nothing that is at a different "level" from that of ordinary existent objects.[5] This consequence of the view Nichols attributes to Reid seems paradoxical only if we adopt "the common prejudice, that every thing which is an object of conception must really exist" (*EIP* V. 5, p. 386).[6]

In short, then, in arguing against the theory of ideas in the *Essays on the Intellectual Powers*, Reid has made a case for the claim that there is nothing about conception, in itself—there is nothing about thinking *of* something—that requires asserting the existence of an object of the act of conception. This is not to deny that some conceptions are of existent things—Reid holds that our perceptions of material objects, for instance, are thoughts about existent things. But a case cannot be made for the theory of ideas simply on the grounds that conception, by its nature, necessarily presupposes the existence of an object of thought. Someone who makes the claim either assumes without justification that there must be causal commerce between the immediate object of thought and the mind, while denying that there need be such interaction between the mind and the mediate object of thought, or else makes the mistake of thinking that content is always supplied by the existence of entities one of which adheres in the other.

Motives Conceived But Non-Existent

Are motives sufficiently analogous to fictional objects or universals to warrant the claim that they too are conceived but non-existent? It's clear

---

[5] In fact, since Reid equates universals with predicables (*EIP* V. 6, p. 393)—that which is predicated of a thing is a universal—his view seems to be that universals, which don't exist, can be predicated of other universals, which also do not exist. Whiteness is conceivable—we can think about it—and in saying this we predicate one universal of another.

[6] There is a question as to how one distinguishes between thoughts about different non-existent objects under this view. What is the difference between a thought about whiteness and a thought about Pegasus? Both, it seems, are thoughts about nothing at all. Perhaps, however, it is no harder to differentiate between non-existent objects than it is to think about them in the first place. Perhaps, that is, this objection arises from the same "common prejudice" that Reid identifies.

enough that we think about fictional objects, and clear enough that we think about things like whiteness or triangularity. It is these facts that present a puzzle, since it is more comfortable to say that such things don't exist than it is to say they do and yet it seems easier to understand how we can think about things that exist than things that don't. But it is difficult to generate a comparable puzzle about motives because, prior to philosophical theorizing about their nature, the term "motive" seems quite correctly to apply to a wide range of things that exist. Pain, for instance, exists, and is naturally described as the motive of efforts to avoid it or alleviate it. Even considerations that exist outside of our minds are quite often motives to act: the proximity of the airline magazine is a large part of what motivates me to read it; it really is close at hand, and that really is part of why I bother to read it. And, of course, desires really exist and they move us to act. How are these intuitive facts to be accomodated by Reid? Or, to put the same question differently, what does Reid think motives are that makes him so confident that they are conceived but do not exist?

An entire essay in the *Essays on the Active Powers* is spent enumerating the various "principles of action" governing human behavior. Reid makes it clear that he uses the term "principles of action" interchangeably with the terms "incitement" and "motive". He writes:

By *principles* of action, I understand every thing that incites us to act.

If there were no incitements to action, active power would be given us in vain. Having no motive to direct our active exertions, the mind would, in all cases, be in a state of perfect indifference, to do this or that, or nothing at all . . . To every action that is of the smallest importance, there must be some incitement, some motive, some reason. (*EAP* III. 1. i, p. 95/543a)[7]

But what exactly does Reid mean by "principles of action"? Reid doesn't offer an explicit definition of the term, but in various places he makes it clear that principles of action are to be equated with either the end for the sake of which an action is performed, or with the thought about that end in virtue of which the agent can be said to be committed to it.[8] Although a

---

[7] It's important to note that Reid's remark here is consistent with his denial that every act is motivated (*EAP* IV. 4, pp. 285–6/609b). What he holds, as the passage makes clear, is that every *non-trivial* act is motivated. An act cannot be worthy of assessment—either moral or otherwise—unless motivated, but he holds that it is nonetheless possible to do trivial things that are nonetheless genuine, unmotivated actions. See Ch. 6 for further discussion.

[8] It is worth noting that the motive of a particular entity's behavior might be an end that is not assigned by the entity, but, instead, by the agent who is acting through the entity. The hammer's motion, for instance, might be motivated by the end of driving the nail; but this motive is

case will be made shortly for thinking his settled position to be the former, for now it is worth nothing that either way Reid is committed to denying that there is a distinct principle of action for each of the various actions that might be performed in order to achieve a given end. Where there is a common end, there is a common principle of action. This point is made clear in a number of passages:

One of the most remarkable acquired desires is that of money, which, in commercial states, will be found in most men, in one degree or other, and, in some men, swallows up every other desire, appetite and passion.

The desire of money can then only be accounted a principle of action, when it is desired for its own sake, and not merely as the means of procuring something else. (EAP III. 2. ii, pp. 135–6/557a–b; see also EAP III. 2. iii, discussed below, and TAC 140)

Reid refuses to call the desire for money as a means to procuring something else a principle of action on the grounds that such a desire is merely instrumental. Therefore, some of the examples offered so far of motives for action would not count as motives, under Reid's view. For instance, pain is only rarely a motive, for Reid. Someone who acts so as to alleviate pain is not motivated by the pain, but by the end of making it stop. Someone who acts so as to avoid future pain is not motivated by the pain, but by the end of avoiding it. By contrast, there are masochists who do act in order to achieve pain. Pain is their motive, under Reid's account, but not because it is an affective push of some sort, but because achieving it constitutes their end. Similarly, circumstances that motivate us to take certain means to our ends—such as the proximity of the airline magazine prompting me to read it—are not motives for Reid. The motive of such an act, the principle of the act, is the end of avoiding boredom, and not those features of the environment in virtue of which reading the magazine serves as a means to that end.

Be that as it may, notice that the remark about the desire for money is consistent with an equation of the principle of action with either a desire that has an end as its object—with, that is, the mental act of thinking of the end as to-be-achieved—or with the object of that desire, the end itself. This ambiguity is recapitulated in other passages. For instance:

[S]ome philosophers, particularly Mr. Hume, think that it is no part of the office of reason to determine the ends we ought to pursue, or the preference due to

---

not the hammer's, but the person's who swings it. Similarly, if an animal acts through instinct, the end at which its behavior aims might be assigned it not by the animal but by the truly active agent behind the animal's behavior, namely, the creator of the animal. So, although instinctive behavior is end-directed, the end in question is not that of the creature whose instinct it is.

one end above another. This, he thinks, is not the office of reason, but of taste or feeling.

If this be so, reason cannot, with any propriety, be called a principle of action. Its office can only be to minister to the principles of action, by discovering the means of their gratification. (*EAP* III. 3. i, p. 202/580*a*)

It is unclear whether, on the view Reid attributes to Hume, Reid takes reason to "minister" to the ends, or to the mental acts (here referred to as "preferences") that take the end as their object.

In other passages, however, he is more naturally read as equating the principle of action with the mental act, rather than its object. For instance:

A thing may be desired either on its own account, or as the means in order to something else. That only can properly be called an object of desire, which is desired upon its own account; and it is only such desires that I call principles of action. When anything is desired as the means only, there must be an end for which it is desired; and the desire of the end is, in this case, the principle of action. The means are desired only as they tend to that end; and if different, or even contrary means tended to the same end, they would be equally desired. (*EAP* III. 2. iii, p. 143/559*b*)

It is the desires that he "call[s] principles of action" and not their objects. However, other passages seem to point in the other direction. They seem, that is, to support the view that Reid equates the principles of action with the end the agent aims to achieve, rather than with the thought by virtue of which he is aiming towards it. For instance: "I understood a motive, when applied to a human being, to be that for the sake of which he acts, and, therefore, that what he was never conscious of, can no more be a motive to determine his will, than it can be an argument to convince his judgment" (*COR* 123, p. 232). It is that which the agent is conscious of, and not the act of being conscious of it, with which Reid here identifies "motives", or, equivalently, principles of action.[9]

It is possible that there is a rational source of this systematic ambiguity in Reid's expression of his position. It is obviously false to claim that any

---

[9] There is a question whether Reid uses the term "conscious" here in the strict sense. Under his official definition of the term, the object of consciousness is always an internal mental state of the agent. Here, however, Reid equates the object of consciousness with that "for the sake of which" one acts. Thus, he seems to be thinking of the object of consciousness as some mind-independent state of affairs. However, someone determined to interpret Reid as equating motives with the mental act of aiming towards an end, rather than with the object of such a thought, might place greater emphasis on Reid's use of the term "consciousness" here than I take the passage to warrant.

end that happens to be furthered by a particular action is the motive for the act. Actions often further ends, even ends to which the agent of the act is committed, despite the fact that the act is not performed for the sake of the end in question. Stopping at the store can further my end of being pleasant to my neighbor, whom I happen to run into in the store as I expected, even if I didn't go to the store in order to be pleasant to my neighbor. What this shows is that identifying the end or ends for the sake of which an act is performed is not merely a matter of identifying the end or ends of the agent that the act actually furthers, and which the agent anticipates furthering through performance of the act. It is extraordinarily difficult to specify with precision what further conditions must be met if an end is to count as the end for the sake of which a particular act is performed. However, it seems clear that the conditions must include something about the way in which the agent conceives of both the end and the act. For an act to be performed for the sake of an end, the agent must think about some intimate relation between the end and the act. (If circularity didn't loom as a result, we might say that the agent must conceive of the end as the motive for the act.) In fact, it is the recognition of something like this point that seems to be animating Reid in the passage just quoted. There he draws the inference that motives must be objects of conscious thought from the fact that they are that for the sake of which acts are performed. This inference doesn't follow unless Reid holds the following, plausible position: *an end is the end for which an act is performed only if the end is thought by the agent to bear some close relation to the act.*

Once this point is recognized it becomes clear how easy it is to slip back and forth between equating the motive for an act with the end itself and equating it with the mental state of the agent by virtue of which the end counts as the end for the sake of which the act is performed. Reid is best understood as consistently equating the motive of an act with the *relevant* end, where the end that is relevant is that end that is thought of by the agent in some special way in virtue of which it counts as the end for the sake of which the act is performed. Under this account, the motive of an act is the object of the relevant mental act, and not the mental act itself. Passages that seem to equate the end with the mental act rather than its object should be understood to be discussing not the motive of an act, but the mental state by virtue of which the relevant motive counts as the motive of the act.

In fact, if Reid's view of motives is to be made consistent with his claim that motives are conceived but non-existent, then he cannot equate motives with the mental acts by virtue of which agents are committed to particular ends. Desires are one such mental act, and there are no principled grounds for Reid to assert either that they are, consistently and without exception, conceived (while we conceive of our desires's objects, we often don't conceive of the desires themselves) or that they are non-existent (they are qualities of our minds). In addition, if motives are equated with the thoughts about our ends, and not the objects of those thoughts, then their non-existence would not need to be established in order to establish that they are not efficient causes: they are thoughts, not things that think, and so cannot have power and exert it. Conversely, if motives are conceived of as the objects of particular mental acts, then it is no easy matter to establish that they are not efficient causes. After all, many things thought about are perfectly capable of having active power and exerting it, and so are capable of being efficient causes. Some further claim would be needed to establish that they are not.

However, if motives are understood on the model that I propose, then there are just as good reasons to take motives to be conceived but non-existent as there are to take either fictional objects or universals to be conceived but non-existent: in all three cases, the sole reason that anyone could have for taking such things to be existent, or for thoughts about them to involve thoughts the objects of which (namely, ideas) exist, is that they are encountered in thought, they are conceived. However, in all three cases, Reid takes this reason to be insufficient. There is nothing about conception itself that requires that its object exists. And, more significantly, there is nothing about the content of our conceptions in any of these three cases that requires that its object exists; we don't think of fictional objects, universals, or ends as necessarily existing: our thoughts about Pegasus are not invalidated, they don't lose their point, if he never was nor will be; our proofs of theorems about triangles are not invalidated if there never was and never will be found an object with three perfectly straight sides; the conception of an act as a means to an end is often rational, and rationally motivates the act, even if the end is never achieved or can't be. In short, the case for thinking that all three classes of entity are non-existent derives in part from the nature of our thoughts about them; in all three cases, the relevant thoughts perform their offices—to help us to tell stories, prove theorems, perform good and evil acts—whether or not their objects exist. Nothing about our thoughts that take these things as objects tell us that they exist. As Reid puts the point with regard to universals, "The conception of whiteness implies no existence; it would remain the same, though every thing in the universe that is white were annihilated" (*EIP* V. 3, p. 367). So, Reid takes the claim that motives are conceived but non-existent to explain why it is that these particular objects of thought, like fictional objects and universals, cannot be efficient causes.

Notice that Reid's case against idealism and skepticism, his case for thinking that material objects exist, also derives from the nature of our thoughts about such objects. Reid repeatedly describes perception as involving a conception of an object *and* a belief that the object exists (cf. *EIP* II. 5, p. 96). It is because perceptions involve this second element—and because they are natural acts of the mind, springing from a fundamental feature of the human constitution—that he takes material objects to exist. Since there is nothing in our thoughts about fictional objects, universals, or ends that involves a presupposition of existence, this form of argument cannot be employed in arguing for the claim that these things exist.

Further, there is no other form of argument that, Reid thinks, will serve to establish the existence of something. With the exception of the existence of God, Reid takes existence claims to be either first principles of some sort, or else to be deducible from first principles at least some of which must, themselves, be existence claims:

The distinction commonly made between abstract truths, and those that express matters of fact, or real existences, coincides in great measure, but not altogether, with that between necessary and contingent truths. The necessary truths that fall within our knowledge are for the most part abstract truths. We must except the existence and nature of the Supreme Being, which is necessary. Other existences are the effects of will and power. They had a beginning, and are mutable. (*EIP* VI. 5, p. 469)

Necessary truths, for Reid, are deducible from necessary first principles; contingent truths are deducible from contingent first principles. In claiming that all true propositions asserting the existence of something (with the exception of the existence of God) are among the contingent truths, Reid implies that they are all deducible, ultimately, from first principles that assert the existence of something. Any true and basic existence claim, any first principle asserting the existence of something, is a proposition that is true only because some entity with power willed that the thing referred to exist. But our justification for belief in such basic existence claims derives only from the nature of our thoughts about the sorts of entities in question; it must be that we believe that the relevant entities exist by virtue of our nature as human beings; there are no other grounds from which to derive a basic existence claim, or any other first principle. But the nature of our conceptions of fictional objects, universals, and ends precludes the possibility of providing an analogous argument for the claim that the propositions asserting their existence are first principles: our natural and non-inferential thoughts about such things make no such presupposition; in conceiving them we don't necessarily conceive them to exist. Since no demonstrative argument could be produced to establish their existence, it follows that an account of the nature of motives, or their relation to behavior, ought not to insist on their existence. The only reasonable view, then, is that they have no more claim to existence than fictional objects or universals.

This chapter began with a pair of questions about Reid's argument for the claim that motives are not efficient causes. What role does the claim that motives are conceived play in that argument? What reasons are there for thinking the claim that motives don't exist to be at all plausible? We are now in a position to provide answers to these questions.

Consider the first question. The claim that motives are conceived is a premise in an argument for the claim that they are not, in their nature, existent things, an argument that is developed explicitly (in so far as it is developed at all) in the discussion not of motives but of other entities that Reid takes to be conceived but non-existent. The motive of an act is an end conceived of as bearing some intimate relation to the act. But since this conception does not presuppose the present or future existence of the end, and since nothing (except God) can be shown to exist except through reflection on our natural thoughts about such things, it follows that there are no grounds for thinking that motives exist. To claim that motives are, by their very nature, the efficient causes of behavior, however, is to claim that the motive of an act *must* exist; it would not count as the motive for the act if it did not. It follows that motives are not efficient causes. The claim that motives are conceived is a crucial step in this argument, informing Reid's readers that he holds the same view of motives that he holds of fictional objects and universals.

But is it at all plausible to think that motives do not exist? Notice that, for all we know, fictional objects and universals exist: maybe Pegasus is roaming about somewhere. But, even if so, there is no reason to believe this *through reflection on the nature of our thoughts about fictional objects or universals.* Someone who insists on the existence of such things, while granting this point, is committed to a more bloated ontology than is required by the nature of his mind. Thus, Reid would see the question of whether or not motives exist as reducing to the question of whether or not there is anything about the thoughts about ends, the thoughts in virtue of which those ends count as the motives of our behavior, that involves a presupposition of the existence of the relevant end. When the question is understood in this way, Reid seems to be quite clearly correct. We often pursue ends precisely because we think that they do not exist, and will not if steps are not taken; and we often pursue ends in the absence of anything like certainty that we will achieve our ends. Further, some ends we recognize to be, in a strict sense, unachievable, even though we think that pursuit of them is worthwhile. This is true of ends that give meaning to our activities quite independently of our attaining them—sometimes the journey really is worth undertaking even if the destination is never reached—but it is also true of some of the most important ends that a human being can pursue such as those to which we are committed by virtue of our traits of character. Recall that, for Reid, a trait of character is a commitment to the instantiation in one's conduct of a particular pattern, or rule. To be wise, for instance, is to be committed to doing things that conform with the rules of wisdom. But at what point has this end been reached? There are always more acts to perform, more opportunities to do things that conform or fail to conform to the rules of wisdom. To be dedicated to following those rules one needn't think that there is some point in one's life at which wisdom has been achieved. The end needn't come to exist in order to give meaning to the activities it structures. Its existence is not what gives our thoughts about it their point.

In full dress, the argument for the claim that motives are not efficient causes, then, should be understood as follows:

(5.1) The motive of an act is the end for the sake of which the act is performed.

(5.2) An act is performed for the sake of a particular end only if the agent thinks about the end.

(5.3) The thought about an end by virtue of which it is the end for the sake of which an act is performed does not presuppose the existence of the end; such thoughts function as they should regardless of whether or not the end thought about exists.

(5.4) With the exception of the existence of God, if a thing exists, then thoughts about it presuppose the thing's existence, or its existence follows from the existence of something else the existence of which is presupposed by such thoughts.

∴ (5.5) Motives do not exist.
(5.6) All efficient causes exist.
∴ Motives are not efficient causes.

Reid should be understood as arguing, then, that a philosopher who claims that the pressure to act under which our motives place us is causal pressure, of the sort exerted by efficient causes, is thereby committed to the claim that the motive for an act exists. But if that existence claim is to be established it must be established as all existence claims (other than the existence of God) are: the existence of the motive must be shown to be either presupposed by our thoughts about motives, or implied by the existence of something else the existence of which those thoughts presuppose. And it is this that Reid denies to be possible.

Conclusion

Once Reid's view of motives and his argument for the claim that motives are not efficient causes are exposed, it can be seen that for Reid the capacity to engage in motivated behavior is a capacity reserved for human beings, and those creatures that lie above us on the Great Chain of Being. Notice, first, that Reid holds, as we have seen in Chapters 1 and 2, that the capacity to direct events towards ends is a capacity reserved for minds. Second, as we have seen in the present chapter, Reid holds that a motive for action is the end for the sake of which the act is performed. Third, as has also been discussed in this chapter, Reid draws a close connection between motives for action, on the one hand, and universals and fictional objects, on the other; in all three cases we have conceptions that do not presuppose, or depend for their point on, the existence of their objects. Motives might be particular (like many fictional objects), or general (like universals), but either way there is nothing about our thoughts about them that presupposes their existence. In addition, fourth, Reid endorses Locke's claim that the capacity for thinking about general categories and kinds of things is the privilege of human beings (cf. Locke, *An Essay Concerning Human Understanding*, II. XI. 10–11; *EIP* V. 5, p. 388). From this collection of views it follows that to be motivated is to exercise the uniquely human capacity to think beyond the province of the existent and to place one's own conduct in the order of ends.

6
The Influence of Motives: The Push of Law?

The fundamental claim on which all naturalistic conceptions of human agency are based is this: the etiology of natural events and the etiology of human actions are of a piece; actions are not, essentially, supernatural. In two obvious senses, Reid's theory of action is naturalistic. First, whether or not a model of human agency is appropriately dubbed "naturalistic" or "non-naturalistic" depends on the story with which it is coupled describing how events in nature come to pass. If we take a mark of the natural, for instance, to be governance by deterministic laws, then any incompatibilist theory of human action will be non-naturalistic; on the other hand, if we allow that even natural events do not always come about in accordance with deterministic laws, then an incompatibilist can advocate a naturalistic position. As a devoted Newtonian, Reid took natural events to come to pass in whatever way a completed Newtonian science describes and he took himself to be following strict Newtonian method in his account of human agency. Since he thought of his own theory of agency as the product of the application of the Newtonian method, he would have taken his theory of agency to be a description of a part of the natural world. Second, and more importantly, Reid holds that both human actions and normal events in nature are the products of the exercise of active power. Thus, for him there is a significant level of metaphysical description under which human actions and natural events are fundamentally the same.

Still, there is an important sense in which Reid's theory of action is non-naturalistic: of all the myriad creatures (excluding God and possibly angels) to whom and within which events take place, only human beings are endowed with active power. And of all the events that take place, only human actions can be traced to active power possessed by the very creatures involved in those events; all other events are traced to exercises of God's active power. Thus, identification of the laws governing events in nature exhausts what there is to be known about the contribution of the finite objects and creatures involved in those events, while identification of the laws governing human actions does not; human beings also contribute active power and its exertion, something that quartz crystals, flowering cacti, jellyfish, and chimpanzees, for instance, do not contribute to the events in which they are involved. Thus Reid advocates a non-naturalistic theory under the following (stipulative) definition of naturalism: *A theory of agency is naturalistic just in case under it the contribution of both natural objects and human beings to the events in which they are involved is exhausted by an account of the laws guiding those events.*[1] According to theories that are naturalistic in this sense, then, to be active is to be a locus of order of a particular kind, order that is captured in an account of the laws according to which the events in question come to pass. To say, for instance, that a bit of behavior is action just in case the person is thereby doing what he wants is to advocate a theory of this sort; such a theory says that a person's contribution to his action consists in robust, law-like links between what he desires and what he does. Even under a view of this sort, there will be differences between human action and ordinary natural events—assuming that jellyfish don't think, they don't want anything, and a thing that doesn't want anything never does what it wants—but the differences are not significant enough to overwhelm the fundamental commonality postulated by any theory of agency that is naturalistic in this sense.

If a naturalistic conception of human agency, in the sense just defined, is correct, it seems virtually certain that the relevant laws linking macro properties of agents and their environments to their behaviors, the laws

[1] Ferenc Huoranszki suggests that the central tenet of the kind of naturalism that Reid takes himself to oppose is the claim that acts of will are reducible to other motives or appetites ("Common Sense and the Theory of Human Behavior", in J. Haldane and S. Read (eds.), *The Philosophy of Thomas Reid* (London: Blackwell Publishing, 2003), 113–30, esp. p. 114). One could deny this claim and still be a naturalist in the sense in which I use the term here. After all, one might agree that acts of will are distinct mental states, irreducible to others, and still think that the contribution of a human being to his action is captured by appeal to laws, for instance, linking his acts of will to his conduct. For another account of the sort of view that Reid takes himself to oppose, see James Harris, "Reid's Challenge to Reductionism About Human Agency", *Reid Studies*, 4/2 (2001), 33–42. Nothing in the naturalistic conception of agency, as just defined, presupposes determinism. If both jellyfish and human beings are indeterministic systems, the contribution of each to their behavior could still be exhausted by the laws governing them; in both cases, the relevant laws would be indeterministic.

that are thought to exhaust human beings's contribution to their actions, will appeal to the motives of agents for acting. It follows that if a naturalistic theory of agency is correct, motives are among the physical causes of human behavior. Reid argues against this claim, and thereby argues against a naturalistic conception of human agency. As he puts the point:

Physicks, in all its branches, is conversant about the phenomena of nature, and their physical causes; and I think it may be admitted as a maxim that every phenomenon of nature has a physical cause. But the actions of men, or of other rational beings, are not phenomena of nature, nor do they come within the sphere of physicks. (COR, app. A, p. 255; see also TAC 183, 185)

The present chapter is concerned with the arguments that Reid offers for the claim that motives are not among the physical causes of human action. In the first, he claims that there is no non-trivial way to specify the particular feature of a motive by virtue of which it is true that it wins the battle with motives for competing actions, and thus there is no non-trivial and yet accurate way to characterize the laws that would govern human behavior were motives physical causes. In the second, he claims that motives cannot, in general, be the physical causes of behavior since we often act without any motive at all. In a third, he argues that there is an analogy between the influence of motives and the influence of advice, and exploits this analogy to show that the influence of motives, like the influence of advice, is not like the influence of physical causes on their physical effects.[2]

Some Preliminaries

Before turning to consideration of the arguments, two preliminary points are in order. First, it might be thought that if the motive of an act is understood as the end at which the agent aims, and by virtue of which the behavior in question counts as action—as has been suggested in Chapter 5—then it is simply obvious that motives are not the physical causes of action. Motives, on this model, might not even exist, and nothing in our thoughts

---

[2] He offers a fourth argument, as well, in the course of his explication of the second: "If a man could not act without any motive, he would have no power at all; for motives are not in our power; and he that has not power over a necessary means, has not power over the end" (EAP IV. 4, p. 286/609b). The fundamental ideas involved in this argument have already been discussed at some length in Ch. 1.

about them presupposes their existence, so how can they be physical causes? However, to object to naturalistic theories of action, under which motives are physical causes, on these grounds would involve a blatant oversimplification of such views. Under such views, the term "motive" refers not to the end but, rather, to the *thought about* the end by virtue of which subsequent behavior counts as action. Such views claim not that the full belly is a physical cause of the filling of it, but, instead, that the *thought of* a full belly as something to be achieved (the desire, choice, or intention favoring that state of affairs) is the physical cause of the relevant behavior. In his attack on the claim that motives are physical causes, Reid puts aside his own official understanding of the nature of motives and employs the term in this way instead. What he is arguing against is the view that human behavior counts as action by virtue of being physically caused by the mental states that account for the end-directedness of that behavior.

In fact, it is important to Reid that motives are not excluded from being physical causes by their very nature, for he takes the motivated behavior of animals to be physically caused (cf. *EAP* IV. 4, p. 289/611*b*). Animal behavior, that is, can be naturalized despite the fact that human behavior cannot be. It follows that Reid's arguments against the claim that human behavior is physically caused must not have equal force against the claim that animal behavior is physically caused. Thus, there is a question that must be answered with respect to any particular argument offered for the claim that motives are not physical causes of human behavior: why doesn't the argument in question apply just as powerfully against the claim that the motives of animals are the physical causes of their behavior? Below, this question will be considered with respect to each of Reid's three arguments.

Another preliminary point: it might seem that Reid's denial of the claim that motives are physical causes is flatly inconsistent with his view of character traits (discussed in Chapter 4). After all, it is essential to Reid's view of character traits that the behavior of an agent who has a character trait follow his motives in accordance with a law. This is clearest in the case of perfectly virtuous beings. For instance, Reid writes: "The most perfect being, in every thing where there is a right and a wrong, a better and a worse, always infallibly acts according to the best motives. This indeed is little else than an identical proposition: for it is a contradiction to say, that a perfect being does what is wrong or unreasonable" (*EAP* IV. 4, p. 284/609*a*). Since an event counts as the physical cause of another just in case the relevant types of events are conjoined by law, it follows that the motives of a perfect being are the physical causes of its behavior; after all, there is a law that says that perfect beings always act on the best motives.[3] But Reid does not consider this to be a counterexample to his claim that motives are not physical causes. Or, rather, it is not a counterexample that threatens the point that Reid really cares about: namely, the refutation of the naturalistic theory of agency. The reason why is that in this case the law in question is authored by the agent: it holds because he has a fixed resolution to act according to a certain rule linking motives with behavior. Or, in other words, the virtuous person's behavior can be subsumed under a law linking behaviors with prior motivation only because the agent exerts his power to act in a consistent, law-like way. As Reid puts the point: "[God's] moral perfection consists in this, that, when he has power to do every thing, a power which cannot be resisted, he exerts that power only in doing what is wisest and best" (EAP IV. 4, pp. 284–5/609a). In short, then, the possibility of regularity in human behavior—and the essential regularity exhibited by conduct expressive of character—is consistent with Reid's arguments against the naturalistic theory of agency. Reid denies that motives are physical causes only in so far as that fact would rule out the possibility that human beings are the efficient causes of their own motivated behavior. The regularity exhibited by action expressive of character, however, does not rule out this possibility but, he thinks, requires it.

Reid considers the importance of the claim that motives are physical causes to derive from the role that it plays in an argument against the non-naturalistic theory of action according to which human beings are endowed with active power. But if a motive's influence can be like the influence of physical causes only if the agent is the author of the law linking motive and behavior—only if, that is, the rule linking one's motives to one's actions holds because of a resolution on one's own part to act according to such a rule—then motives have physical-causal influence only if the behavior they motivate is efficiently caused by the agent. Such a result favors, rather than opposes, Reid's view of human action as essentially different from ordinary natural change.

An Argument from the Concept of Motivational Strength

One way to make good on the claim that motives are among the physical causes of action is to identify a law that does, in fact, link an agent's motives

---

[3] Reid describes the claim that a perfect being acts on the best motives as "an identical proposition". This implies that it is an uninformative tautology, and thus, as stated, is not a law of nature, for laws of nature are, in Kantian terms, synthetic, not analytic. So understood, the term "a perfect being" is being read *de dicto*. Read *de re*, the statement is not "an identical proposition" and is a law governing the behavior of the particular being that happens to be perfect.

with his behavior (and which is not authored by the agent himself). We might think, for instance, that human beings always act on their strongest motive; there is a constant conjunction, we might say, between a motive's being the strongest and its prevailing. Reid summarizes his objection to this claim as follows:

It is a question of fact, whether the influence of motives be fixed by laws of nature, so that they shall always have the same effect in the same circumstances. Upon this, indeed, the question about liberty and necessity hangs. But I have never seen any proof that there are such laws of nature, far less any proof that the strongest motive always prevails. However much our late fatalists have boasted of this principle as of a law of nature, without ever telling us what they mean by the strongest motive, I am persuaded that, whenever they shall be pleased to give us any measure of the strength of motives distinct from their prevalence, it will appear, from experience, that the strongest motive does not always prevail. If no other test or measure of the strength of motives can be found but their prevailing, then this boasted principle will be only an identical proposition, and signify only that the strongest motive is the strongest motive, and the motive that prevails is the motive that prevails—which proves nothing.   (*COR* 93, pp. 176–7)

Reid's point, then, is that depending how "strength" is defined, the claim that we always act on the strongest motive will either be trivial (an "identical proposition") or false. In the *Essays on the Active Powers*, in which the argument summarized here is expressed at large, Reid offers four distinct accounts of strength of motivation. The first account simply equates the strongest motive with the motive on which the agent acts (*EAP* IV. 4, p. 287/610*b*):

> *Strength as Prevalence*: S's motive to A is the strongest of his motives *if and only if* S As.

As Reid points out, under the account of Strength as Prevalence, to say that the agent acted on the strongest of his motives is to say no more than that he acted. Since his acting is consistent both with his action being physically caused by his motives and not being physically caused by them, the truth of the relevant law in this case does not tell us anything about the truth or falsity of naturalistic theories of action.

The second account of strength of motivation is a bit more difficult to characterize. Reid describes it this way:

[It might] be said, that by strength of a motive is not meant its prevalence, but the cause of its prevalence; that we measure the cause by the effect, and from the superiority of the effect conclude the superiority of the cause, as we conclude that to be the heaviest weight which bears down the scale.   (*EAP* IV. 4, p. 288/610*b*)

Reid's idea here seems to be that one might think that strength is a property of a motive that we *know of* only through the physical effects the motive has. We don't think that the heaviness of the heavier of two weights *consists* in its sitting on the side of the scale that tips; rather, we think that the fact that it sits on that side of the scale indicates that it possesses the property of being the heavier of the two. The property of being the heavier of the two weights is decisively indicated, but not equated with, the property of tipping the scale. Put formally, this account of strength can be understood as follows:

> *Strength as the Basis of Prevalence*: S's motive to A is the strongest of his motives *if and only if* the motive has some property accounting for the fact that S As and we can know it to have that property if S As.

Reid thinks that this account of strength serves the aims of those who take motives to be physical causes no better than the first account. He writes:

> [A]ccording to this explication of the axiom [namely, that people always act on the strongest motive], it takes for granted that motives are the causes, and the sole causes of actions. Nothing is left to the agent, but to be acted upon by the motives, as the balance by the weights. The axiom supposes, that the agent does not act, but is acted upon; and, from this supposition, it is concluded that he does not act. This is to reason in a circle, or rather it is not reasoning but begging the question. (*EAP* IV. 4, p. 288/610*b*)

Reid is claiming that someone who holds the account of Strength as the Basis of Prevalence, can only defend the claim that people always act on their strongest motives by asserting it, and thus reasoning in a circle.

But why does Reid think there's a circle here? Consider Reid's own analogy. Imagine someone who claims that the heaviest weight always tips the scale and, when asked to define "heaviest", answers that the heaviest weight is the one endowed with property H; he goes on to say that, as it happens, we know if a weight has that property by seeing if it tips the scale. Has this person reasoned in a circle? No, although he hasn't offered an adequate justification for the claim that the heaviest weight always tips the scale. He hasn't reasoned in a circle because he doesn't equate property H with the tipping of the scale; he doesn't say that the weights with property H tip the scale because they tip the scale. Rather, he says they tip the scale because they have property H, and he makes no effort to explain why weights with that property tip the scale. Still, the claim that the weight with property H always tips the scale is empirically empty: the evidence that would support the view that a particular weight has property H and the evidence that would support the claim that the weight with that property tips the scale are the same. The result is that epistemic principles regarding the independence of evidence are violated by someone who claims to have evidence that the heaviest weight tips the scale, but uses the same evidence to determine which weights are heaviest. This doesn't show it to be false that the heaviest weight tips the scale, or even necessarily empirically unjustifiable: were a method for detecting property H invented that didn't involve checking a weight to see if it tips the scale, then it could be empirically confirmed that the heaviest weight tips the scale. Similarly, if a method could be devised for assessing whether or not a motive is the strongest, under the view of Strength as the Basis of Prevalence, that did not require determining if the agent acts on it, then it could be empirically verified that agents always act on the strongest motive.

So, Reid overstates his point slightly in accusing the advocate of the view of Strength as the Basis of Prevalence of reasoning in a circle. What he should say is that someone who adopts the view of Strength as the Basis of Prevalence can only avoid begging the question against those who deny that people always act on the strongest motive by first offering an independent way of identifying the strongest motive. In fact, this is almost exactly what he does say two paragraphs later in summarizing the argument up to this point:

> We are therefore brought to this issue, that unless some measure of strength of motives can be found distinct from their prevalence, it cannot be determined, whether the strongest motive always prevails or not. If such a measure can be found and applied, we may be able to judge of the truth of this maxim, but not otherwise. (*EAP* IV. 4, p. 288/611*a*)

The point here is epistemic, not metaphysical. What is required is not an account of the nature of the strongest motive, but rather a method of *measuring* to determine if a particular motive is the strongest one, a method that does not require determining if that motive prevails.

In fact, the next two accounts of strength of motive that Reid offers— under which, he thinks, it is non-trivial, but false, to say that we always act on the strongest motive—are intended as prevalence-independent methods of determining if a particular motive is the strongest. He writes:

> Hunger is a motive in a dog to eat; so is it in a man. According to the strength of the appetite, it gives a stronger or a weaker impulse to eat. And the same thing may be said of every other appetite and passion. Such animal motives give an impulse to

the agent, to which he yields with ease; and, if the impulse be strong, it cannot be resisted without an effort which requires a greater or a less degree of self-command. Such motives are not addressed to the rational powers. Their influence is immediately upon the will. We feel their influence, and judge of their strength, by the conscious effort which is necessary to resist them.   (*EAP* IV. 4, p. 289/611a–b)

Reid here appeals to an unanalyzed notion of strength of *appetite* in the proposed account of strength of motive: the motive to eat is strong or weak to the degree to which the appetite for food is strong or weak. Earlier in the *Essays on the Active Powers*, Reid has identified a defining feature of appetites: "Every appetite is accompanied with an uneasy sensation proper to it, which is strong or weak, in proportion to the desire we have of the object" (*EAP* III. 2. i, p. 119/551b). By appealing to an "uneasy" sensation, Reid is explicitly signaling his readers that he is using the concept of "uneasiness" developed by Locke. Locke writes: "All pain of the body of what sort soever, and disquiet of the mind, is *uneasiness*: And with this is always join'd Desire, equal to the pain or *uneasiness* felt; and is scarce distinguishable from it" (*Essay Concerning Human Understanding*, II. XXI. 31). To be uneasy is to feel pain in the absence of something; uneasiness is the pain felt as a result of something being absent from one's current state. It is clear enough how pain can admit of greater or less, and so uneasinesses can be more or less severe; they can be stronger or weaker pains. So, Reid's idea seems to be that, in the sense proposed, a motive is strong to the degree to which it hurts to resist doing what it dictates. That is, the stronger the uneasiness in the absence of what the motive dictates, the stronger the motive. It is through the immediate consciousness of the pain that will be felt should we fail to act as dictated by a particular motive that we determine whether or not it is the strongest. This is what Reid calls "the animal test" of motivational strength (*EAP* IV. 4, p. 289/611b); it is a way of identifying the strength of a motive independently of the motive's prevalence. More formally, we can think of Reid as offering the following account of strength of motive:

> *Strength as the Pain of Resistance*: S's motive to A is the strongest of his motives *if and only if* the prospect of not A-ing is attended with greater uneasiness for S than the prospect of not performing any one of his other actions.

Under this test, a motive is not strongest simply because doing something other than what it dictates will result in the most pain for the agent. For one thing, the agent might not know that acting contrary to a motive will cause great pain, and so the prospect of the action might be attended with no uneasiness. In addition, the prospect of an action that will cause very great pain, and is expected to by the agent, might not be attended by uneasiness as strong as the pain that will be felt. An agent might, for instance, "discount" future pains—anticipate them in his uneasinesses as less than they will be—or might feel greater uneasiness for one kind of pain, say emotional pain, than for comparable amounts of other kinds of pain, say physical pain.

Still, in the account of Strength as the Pain of Resistance, the strength of a motive reduces to the strength of a correlative state: the state of uneasiness attending the prospect of non-performance of the act dictated by the motive. Similarly, in what Reid calls the "rational test" of the strength of a motive, the strength of a motive reduces to the "strength" of another correlated state: the state of judgment of the overall value of the end in question. He writes:

[Rational motives'] influence is upon the judgment, by convincing us that such an action ought to be done, that it is our duty, or conducive to our real good, or to some end which we have determined to pursue. . . .

If there be any competition between rational motives it is evident, that the strongest, in the eye of reason, is that which it is most our duty and our real happiness to follow. (*EAP* IV. 4, p. 290/611*b*–612*a*)

Here Reid is proposing the last of the four accounts of strength of motive:

Strength as Judged Optimality: S's motive to A is the strongest of his motives *if and only if* S judges A to be, all things considered, the best of his possible actions.

Just as Locke claims that one's uneasinesses can point in a direction that conflicts with one's judgment about what is best to do (*Essay Concerning Human Understanding*, II. XXI. 35), Reid claims that the motive that is strongest in the sense of Strength as the Pain of Resistance is not necessarily the strongest in the sense of Strength as Judged Optimality. However, Reid has an importantly different view from Locke's in another respect: Locke holds that we always choose as dictated by our strongest uneasinesses, and holds also that our choices are influenced by our judgments about what's best only to the degree to which we raise uneasinesses in ourselves that accord with those judgments (*Essay Concerning Human Understanding*, II. XXI. 40, II. XXI. 45–6).[4] But Reid holds, instead, that we often

---

[4] This oversimplifies Locke's view slightly. He holds that the strongest uneasiness does not lead to action when it points to something judged by the agent to be unattainable (*Essay Concerning Human Understanding*, II. XXI. 40).

act in accordance with our judgments, and contrary to our uneasinesses. We often do what we judge to be right, that is, even if we anticipate that it will hurt more to do it than it would hurt to do something else. To act in accordance with judgment, Reid thinks, contrary to Locke, we need not raise uneasinesses in ourselves that point in the same direction as our judgment.

This difference between Locke and Reid amounts to the difference between two different models of strong-willed conduct. For both Locke and Reid, the *weak*-willed person judges A to be his best act, but chooses in accordance with uneasinesses pointing away from A. For Locke, the strong-willed person must "correct" his uneasinesses—he must develop uneasinesses that accord with his judgment, if he is to act correctly. But for Reid, the strong-willed person simply chooses on the basis of his judgment. His judgment can play an uneasiness-independent role in the etiology of his conduct. So, while the claim that we always act on the strongest motive, when strength is interpreted either as Pain of Resistance or as Judged Optimality, is non-trivial, Reid also takes it to be false since we sometimes act as dictated by judgment, sometimes as dictated by uneasiness, and the two often come apart. If weak-willed conduct is possible, in the sense in which both Locke and Reid understand it, then we do not always act in accord with the motive strongest according to the rational test; if strong-willed conduct is possible, in the sense in which Reid, but not Locke, understands it, then we do not always act in accord with the motive strongest according to the animal test. Since Reid thinks both kinds of conduct are not just possible but common, he concludes that we do not always act according to the strongest motive in either sense of "strength".

It is worth noting that Reid does not claim that we sometimes judge an action to be the best of our options, and do it, while lacking any feeling, or uneasiness, that points in its direction. One set of judgments of optimality is moral judgments, and Reid is clear that although moral judgments are genuine judgments—they can be true or false—they are always accompanied by a feeling: "When I exercise my moral faculty about my own actions or those of other men, I am conscious that I judge as well as feel" (*EAP* V. 7, p. 464/673*a*). It seems that Reid holds that when one does an act, judging it to be the morally required act, one does get some kind of pleasure that serves to offset the pain experienced by acting contrary to uneasinesses that point away from the act performed. However, this by itself does not imply that the agent would experience more pain by acting contrary to his judgment than he would by acting on any other motive. That is, it does not imply that his motive to act morally is strongest under the view of Strength as the Pain of Resistance.

However, Reid also holds that the feeling that accompanies moral judgment is "regulated" by that judgment. Discussing what happens when he sees "a man exerting himself nobly in a good cause", Reid writes:

> I am . . . conscious, that this agreeable feeling in me, and this esteem of him, depend entirely upon the judgment I form of his conduct. I judge that this conduct merits esteem; and while I thus judge, I cannot but esteem him, and contemplate his conduct with pleasure. Persuade me that he was bribed, or that he acted from some mercenary or bad motive, immediately my esteem and my agreeable feeling vanish. (*EAP* V. 7, p. 463/673*a*)

If the feeling that accompanies the judgment of optimality is not strongest under the view of Strength as the Pain of Resistance, then the way in which the judgment regulates the accompanying feeling must be complex. In particular, Reid cannot hold that the judgment regulates the feeling in the following way: the better the act is judged to be, the stronger the accompanying feeling in its favor. If he were to hold this, then he would be committed to the claim that agents do, in fact, always act on the motive that it hurts least to resist. Instead, he must hold that the strength of the feeling that accompanies the judgment of optimality and is regulated by it, while partly a function of the content of the judgment, is determined by other factors as well; it cannot be strongest simply because the act it favors is judged to be optimal.[5]

Be that as it may, if we grant that we sometimes act in accord with our judgments, even when we anticipate suffering more pain as a result than we would by acting contrary to them, and yet we sometimes act on the motive strongest in the sense of Strength as the Pain of Resistance, even when it conflicts with our judgment regarding what act is best, then it follows that we do not always act on the strongest motive in either of the two relevant senses. But it does not follow that there is no law linking our motives with our subsequent behavior. One might think that Reid admits that the following generality is true: people always act on the motive that is strongest in *one* of the two senses. In fact, since Reid holds that we sometimes act without any motive at all (a claim to be discussed in the next

---

[5] This immediately raises the question of exactly what relationship the strength of the relevant feeling bears to the judgment it accompanies. Since Reid is primarily concerned to refute the point that moral judgments are not properly judgments at all (a point that he attributes, perhaps unjustly, to Hume), he makes little progress on this question.

section), he denies even this disjunction.[6] Still, as noted already, Reid admits that animals always act on the motive strongest in the sense of Pain of Resistance (cf. *EAP* IV. 4, p. 289/611b); this is why the argument from the concept of motivational strength only shows, Reid thinks, that human behavior is not physically caused, and does not apply promiscuously to animal behavior. This might lead us to think that at least in the case in which a person has no competing rational motive—no motive the strength of which is to be measured on the scale of Judged Optimality—but does have competing animal motives, that the person will act on the motive strongest in the sense of Pain of Resistance. Perhaps, that is, Reid's belief that animal behavior can be naturalized commits him to holding that the following, albeit limited, law governs human behavior: if a person has conflicting animal motives, and no relevant rational motives, he will act on the motive strongest in the sense of Pain of Resistance. If this is true, then at least in one set of cases, our motives are, indeed, among the physical causes of our behavior.

If Reid allows this result, then he is committed to denying that human beings are the efficient causes of their behavior when they have no rational motives. This would further commit him to the claim that in such cases, people are not responsible for their conduct.[7] Determining how Reid would respond to this problem requires interpreting a phrase that he uses in a variety of contexts: "self-command". For instance, consider the following passage:

When a man is acted upon by contrary motives of this kind [that is, animal motives], he finds it easy to yield to the strongest [in the sense of Pain of Resistance]. They are like two forces pushing him in contrary directions. To yield to the strongest, he needs only to be passive. By exerting his own force, he may resist ... [T]hat is the strongest of contrary motives, to which he can yield with ease, or which it requires an effort of self-command to resist. (*EAP* IV. 4, p. 289/611b)

If it is possible to exercise one's "self-command" in favor of an act the motive for which is less than the strongest in the sense of Pain of Resistance *even if that act is not favored by any rational motive*, then Reid is denying that when an agent lacks any relevant rational motive, his strongest animal

---

[6] Even if this disjunction were true, there is a question as to whether or not any disjunctive generality can count as a law. Laws of nature, we might say, are not disjunctions.

[7] The same issue arises in relation to Kant's moral psychology. If we are responsible only when we act autonomously, and if all action on the basis of inclination is not autonomous, then agents seem to be non-responsible whenever they act on inclination. This issue has been discussed extensively in the secondary literature on Kant. For a start, see Onora Nell, *Acting on Principle: An Essay on Kantian Ethics* (New York: Columbia University Press, 1975).

motive is the physical cause of his behavior. On the other hand, perhaps in this passage Reid is imagining that in exercising his self-command the agent is thereby complying with a rational motive strongest in the sense of Judged Optimality. If this is his view, then the passage doesn't address the case under consideration, namely, the case in which the agent has only competing animal motives and no relevant rational motive.[8]

However, in other contexts it becomes clear that Reid does allow the possibility of exercising one's self-command so as to act on less than the strongest animal motive even in the absence of any rational motive favoring the performed act. He offers us a thought experiment: "[W]e may take a complex view of [the animal motive's] effect in life, by supposing a being actuated by principles of no higher order, to have no conscience or sense of duty, only let us allow him that superiority of understanding, and that power of self-government which man actually has" (*EAP* III. ii. 8, p. 196/578*a*). For the imagined being to even be possible, it must be possible to have the power of self-government without having any rational motives. Further, Reid goes on to make the following claim, which is quite striking in this context: "Without self-government, that [motive] which is strongest at the time will prevail. And that which is the weakest at any one time may, from passion, from a change of disposition or of fortune, become strongest at another time" (*EAP* III. ii. 8, p. 197/578*b*). Thus, Reid seems to hold that the difference between a person who has only animal motives, on the one hand, and an animal, on the other, is that a person has the power to act on an animal motive that is less than the strongest in the sense of Pain of Resistance; people have the power of "self-government" even when lacking any rational motives. On this basis, Reid would deny that motives are physical causes of human behavior even when there is no competing rational motive on which to act. However, Reid provides us with no satisfactory reason for drawing a distinction between animals and people in this regard. He doesn't provide us with any satisfactory reason for believing that people have the power of "self-command" independently of our capacity for rational motivation.

Although Reid's position on this issue is hardly principled, less turns on it, for our purposes, than might appear. If there are any cases of motivated

---

[8] Although he doesn't specifically discuss this passage, Knud Haakonsen commits himself to this reading by claiming that, for Reid, "[m]oral freedom is . . . a matter of being able or competent to judge of what it is one is willing" (Thomas Reid, *Practical Ethics*, ed. K. Haakonsen (Princeton: Princeton University Press, 1990), 45). What follows in the main text is a brief argument against this interpretation.

behavior that cannot be subsumed under law, then motives are not always among the physical causes of action, and Reid's anti-naturalism is defended. So, even if Reid admits that motives are among the physical causes of human behavior in the absence of rational motives, he might still insist that there is a large class of cases of motivated behavior that cannot be subsumed under law, namely, those in which a person's motive strongest in the sense of Pain of Resistance points towards a different act from that favored by his motive strongest in the sense of Judged Optimality. However, even in the case in which there is conflict between the motive strongest in the one sense and the motive strongest in the other there may be some further feature of the motives in question that determines which motive prevails. The strongest rational motive might be stronger than the strongest animal motive, or vice versa, in some sense of "strength" that is yet to be identified, and in that sense it might be quite true that we always act on the strongest motive. The portion of argument so far reconstructed, that is, does not indicate principled grounds for thinking that, across the board, there are no laws linking motives with subsequent behavior—laws by virtue of which motives count as the physical causes of behavior—but only grounds for thinking that the particular law, "People always act on the strongest motive", when interpreted in any of the four ways Reid considers, is not the law under which human behavior is to be subsumed. This is not a result by which naturalists about human action, those who think that human behavior is physically caused by motives, ought to feel threatened. In the end, it amounts to little more than the welcome result that the laws governing the role of motives in the generation of behavior that capture the distinctive contribution of a human being to his action, if there are any, must be somewhat more complicated than one might have thought.

However, to assert that there is some law linking motives with behavior—or, what's the same thing, that there is some conception of strength of motivation under which it is both non-trivial and true that people always act on the strongest of their motives—is not to specify the law in question. Rather, it is to appeal to the existence of unknown physical causes, or rather to unknown features of motives by virtue of which they are the physical causes of behavior. In fact, Reid addresses this version of the view that motives are the physical causes of action. Commenting on a manuscript sent him by James Gregory, he writes:

That motives are the sole causes of action, is only an outwork in the system of Necessity, and may be given up, while it is maintained that every action must have a physical cause; for physical causes of all human actions, whether they be known or unknown, are equally inconsistent with liberty.

A physical cause, from its nature, must be constant in its effects, when it exists, and is applied to its proper object. But of unknown causes, the existence and the application may depend upon a concurrence of accidents, which is not subject to calculation, or even to rational conjecture. So that, I apprehend, the existence of such causes can never be demonstrated to be contrary to matter of fact. Unknown causes, like occult qualities, suit every occasion, and can never be contradicted by phaenomena; for, as we cannot, *a priori*, determine what shall be the effects of causes absolutely unknown; so it is impossible to prove, of any effect whatsoever, that it cannot be produced by some unknown physical cause or causes.   (*COR*, app. A, p. 258)

The point that Reid is making here is closely allied to his objection to the claim that people always act on the strongest motive under the view of Strength as the Basis of Prevalence. Under that view, the concept of strength becomes a stand-in for whatever property of motives is nomically conjoined with compliant behavior; without some independent means of apprehending that property, the claim that we always act on the strongest motive is without justification. Similarly, to assert that there is some collection of antecedents of action that are nomically conjoined with action, without specifying the nature of those antecedents, is to employ a dummy concept; we might as well simply announce that the strongest motive is the one that figures in the conditions, whatever they are, that are nomically conjoined with action and thereby emptily defend the claim that people always act on the strongest motive.

What is left of Reid's argument from the concept of motivational strength when the possibility of probabilistic laws is introduced?[9] After all, we might say, a law like "If motive M is strongest in the sense of Strength as Judged Optimality, then S will act on M 70 per cent of the time" might be true, for all Reid says, and hence it would follow that there is a law linking a motive's strength with its prevalence. This question is important, since Reid's anti-naturalism is just as threatened by the possibility of probabilistic laws governing human behavior as it is by deterministic laws. If there is a law governing a person's behavior, and the law is not authored by the person himself, then he is not the efficient cause of his behavior; rather, the efficient cause of his behavior is whatever entity it is whose resolution accounts for the truth of the relevant law; this is true regardless of

---

[9] John Fischer helped me to see the importance of this question.

whether or not the law is probabilistic or deterministic. Even if God flips a coin before deciding whether to make it the case that a person does what he judges to be best, it is still God who is the efficient cause of the person's behavior, and not the person himself.

There is a temptation to say that, in allowing that people always act on either the motive strongest in the sense of Pain of Resistance, or strongest in the sense of Judged Optimality, Reid thereby allows that there is some probabilistic law linking a motive's strength with its prevalence. After all, we might say, whatever the actual distribution of instances in which people act on their motive strongest in the one sense, or their motive strongest in the other, there is a corresponding probabilistic law linking motives and behavior. This is a mistake, however, deriving from a mistake in the understanding of a probabilistic *law*. To see this, note first that there is a long-standing, and very difficult philosophical problem of how precisely to distinguish a law of nature from other true, synthetic generalities. In fact, Reid is one of the first really to press this problem in his famous criticism of Hume's theory of causation: "It follows from [Hume's] definition of a cause, that night is the cause of day, and day the cause of night. For no two things have more constantly followed each other since the beginning of the world" (*EAP* IV. 9, p. 334/627a). What the objection shows is that constant conjunction isn't sufficient for nomic conjunction. We need a better measure of whether or not a generality is a law. This is just as true with respect to probabilistic laws: the mere fact that two kinds of event are conjoined together x per cent of the time does not show that there is a law saying that when the first occurs the second will occur x per cent of the time. So, even if it were true that people act on the motive strongest in the sense of Pain of Resistance x per cent of the time, it would not follow that there was a corresponding probabilistic law governing the motive–action connection.

Determining whether or not a particular data set does, in fact, support the claim that a particular probabilistic law is true, then, is a subtle matter, and not simply reducible to the question of whether or not the data is distributed as would be expected, were the relevant law true. Conversely, probabilistic laws are much more difficult to falsify than deterministic laws, since single deviations from the pattern the law specifies are consistent with the truth of the law. So, the mere fact that people sometimes act as they judge to be best, sometimes as their uneasinesses dictate, simply doesn't show *either* that there is, or is not, a probabilistic law governing human behavior. The important point, however, on which Reid would wish to place emphasis, is that those who claim that there is a probabilistic law connecting motives with behavior need to collect data about motivated behavior, and need to show us that the data does indeed support the assertion of the relevant probabilistic law. It is not the results of such difficult empirical work that fuels the confidence of those who take there to be laws, even probabilistic laws, linking motivational strength with prevalence.

The point that lies at the heart of Reid's argument from the concept of motivational strength is this: commitment to a naturalistic conception of human agency, which manifests itself, for Reid, in the claim that all action is physically caused, rarely derives from the legitimate empirical discovery of laws governing human behavior. Naturalistic commitments usually derive, instead, from a dissatisfaction with the alternative and with the sense, legitimate or not, that there is a degree of intelligibility that the natural sciences can give to the phenomena they investigate that it would be desirable to have with respect to human behavior. But this is no argument for the view that human action is physically caused. That argument is best made through the articulation of laws that can be legitimately, empirically, shown to govern human behavior. As the sciences of human behavior develop, there may be more and more reason for the naturalist to be optimistic. Still, what Reid's argument from the concept of motivational strength shows is that discoveries made from the armchair provide little by way of non-trivial support for the naturalistic conception of human agency. As obvious as it seems that we act on the strongest of our motives, it is difficult, if not impossible, to make sense of this obvious truth without sinking it into triviality.

A Lesson from Buridan's Ass

Where Reid's argument from the concept of motivational strength attacks a particular plausible form of the claim that motives are physical causes—the form in which the relevant law linking motives and behavior appeals to the strength of the antecedent motive—his second argument attacks the claim in whatever form it might take; that is, it attacks the claim that there is any law at all linking motives and subsequent behavior. The central claim of the argument is very straightforward: motives aren't the physical causes of all action because we often act without any motive at all.

In defense of the claim that we often act without any motive at all, Reid identifies a class of cases in which, he thinks, agents act without any motive for what they do. He writes:

Cases frequently occur, in which an end, that is of some importance, may be answered equally well by any one of several different means. In such cases, a man who intends the end finds not the least difficulty in taking one of these means, though he be firmly persuaded, that it has no title to be preferred to any of the others.

To say that this is a case that cannot happen, is to contradict the experience of mankind; for surely a man who has occasion to lay out a shilling, or a guinea, may have two hundred that are of equal value, both to the giver and to the receiver, any one of which will answer his purpose equally well.   (*EAP* IV. 4, pp. 285–6/609b)

Since Reid holds that animals are physically caused to act by their motives, he must think it impossible to construct cases of the sort that he identifies here with respect to animal behavior. He must think, that is, that Buridan's ass really would starve, even though a person, placed in the same situation, would not. However, even with respect to human beings, the moral that Reid wishes to draw from the cases he identifies here—namely, that they are cases in which we act without any motive—is not clearly justified. Since, for Reid, all genuine action is end-directed, he cannot deny that the man who hands over one of the many identical shillings in his pocket is not engaging in an end-directed activity and at the same time assert that the man's behavior is action. The man is aiming to pay someone a shilling, and it is in part because of the fact that his behavior is aimed at that end that it counts as action, as the exercise of active power. Since, for our purposes in this chapter, motives are being equated with the thoughts about ends by virtue of which behaviors count as aimed towards those ends, it seems that Reid is committed to saying that the man does, in fact, have a motive for his action: the man's commitment to the end of paying a shilling is what motivates him to pay with whatever shilling he selects. The point applies generally, it would seem, to all of the cases of the sort that Reid identifies. If a person adopts one of the many equivalently good means to his end, he still aims at the end, and is therefore still motivated to do what he does.[10]

As Reid notes, in the passage just quoted, what people lack in cases of the sort that he describes is any motive favoring the act performed over

---

[10] The point being made here is really just the point on the tip of the tongue of anyone confronted for the first time with Buridan's ass. Of course the ass has a motive to take one bale of hay over the other! If he doesn't take one, he'll starve.

a variety of other acts; the man has no motive for giving *this* shilling, rather than *that* shilling, although he has a motive to give *a* shilling. We could try to develop this point into an argument against the claim that motives are the physical causes of action like so. We might say that all the laws in virtue of which a particular event or state count as action are strictly deterministic: in every case of physical causation, given the physical cause, a particular, singular, physical effect must follow. Since, given the very same set of motives, any one of the various equivalently good means to its satisfaction might be adopted, it follows that motives are not linked to action in the way that physical causes are linked to their physical effects.

There are two problems with this strategy. First, as an interpretive matter, it is fairly clear that this is not what Reid has in mind. He takes the moral of his cases to be that we sometimes act with no motive at all; he doesn't take the moral to be that motives for action underdetermine what action the agent will perform. Second, and more importantly, understood in this way the cases that Reid describes would, at best, show that a putative law of the form "If S is motivated to A, then S As" is false since there are perfectly good means to one's end that one does not adopt despite having some motive to do so. But we hardly need to appeal to those cases to establish that: when we are motivated to do more than one incompatible thing, we often leave one of the things we are motivated to do undone. This doesn't show anything of great importance: there very well might be some feature of the motive that prevails that is nomically linked to the behavior performed in accordance with it, such as the motive's degree of strength. In short, so understood Reid's argument here would depend, ultimately, on the success of the argument from the concept of motivational strength, and he clearly intends the argument under consideration to establish his anti-causalist conclusion independently.

So, the question is this: why does Reid think that cases of the sort that he describes involve action without a motive, given that he clearly takes such actions to be end-directed? Since end-directed actions are all of them motivated, in a sense, Reid must think that in the cases of the sort that he identifies there is no motive *of the sort that can serve as a physical cause*. But what sort of thing must a motive be to serve as a physical cause? And what reasons are there to think that, in the sorts of cases Reid identifies, the agent acts without such a motive?

To answer these questions, it helps to look at what Reid has to say about an example originally developed by James Gregory. A porter is offered a guinea per mile to take a letter from point A to point B, and independently

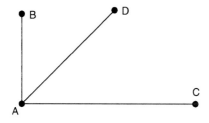

Figure 1. AB is half the length of AC. AD is three-quarters the length of AC. The porter is offered the same amount of money to travel from A to B as from A to C.

offered a half-guinea per mile to take a letter from point A to point C, twice as far away (see Figure 1). Assuming that the porter can't accept both offers, and assuming that the only motive to act is monetary—the porter doesn't care about the extra distance required to travel to point C—the porter seems to have equal incentive to accept the one offer as he does to accept the other. The question is what, if anything, the porter will do. Reid responds to the example in a letter to Gregory. He writes:

> One should think that the [motive to travel to point B and the motive to travel to point C], would conjoyn their force in the diagonal [thus leading the porter to travel to point D in Figure 1]. But, by going in the diagonal, he loses both the guineas and the half-guineas; this is implied in the offer, and is a motive not to go in the diagonal, as strong as the two motives for going in it. By the force of the two motives, he must *will* to go in the diagonal; by the force of the third, he must *will* not to go in the diagonal.
>
> You pretend to demonstrate that he must go in the diagonal willingly. I think it may be demonstrated, with equal force, that he must will not to go in the diagonal. I perceive no error in either demonstration; and, if both demonstrations be good, what must be the conclusion? The conclusion must be, that the supposition on which both demonstrations are grounded must be false—I mean the supposition that motives are the physical causes of actions; for it is possible, and often happens, that, from a false supposition, two contradictory conclusions may be drawn; but, from a true supposition, it is impossible.   (*COR*, app. A, p. 257)

The example is silly. Still, a lesson can be drawn about the way in which Reid conceives of the examples that he takes to illustrate that we sometimes act without any motive at all from his treatment of Gregory's example. In Gregory's example, the porter has the end of getting the money and recognizes that he has two incompatible means for reaching it, between which he is indifferent: travel to point B or travel to point C. Thus, this is an example of just the sort that Reid takes to illustrate the possibility of action without a motive. So, we would expect Reid to say that should the porter opt to travel, say, to point B, that he would have no motive to do so, despite the fact that by doing so he achieves his end of getting the money. However, as Reid notes in his discussion of the example, he takes the porter to have motive not to do anything that will result in his failure to get the money—such as travelling to point D—and he takes this third motive to be as strong as the *combination* of the other two motives. So, Reid grants that the motive to travel to point B and the motive to travel to point C combine to produce a motive to do something else entirely: travel to point D. That is, he seems to grant that the two motives add together in some way and thus that the agent is, in fact, motivated to travel to point D.

It is clearly an absurd view of the influence of motives—absurd enough never to have been held by anyone—under which it follows that the porter is motivated to travel to point D. This would make sense only if motivational forces are thought to be additive in just the way in which physical forces are, in accordance with the rules of the vector calculus. But only someone who takes the analogy between motivational forces and physical forces far too seriously would agree to this, and those who hold that motives are physical causes of action are not thereby committed to it. Still, it is not nearly so absurd to think that motives to do incompatible things combine in *some* way, even if the rules of combination are not the same as the rules of combination of physical forces. It is natural to think that there is such a thing as what one is motivated to do *all-things-considered*; all-things-considered motivation is what results when prima facie motives favoring various actions combine in whatever way in which it makes sense to think of them as combining.[11] Perhaps it is this to which Reid takes someone who holds motives to be physical causes to be committed: *all of an agent's motives to act combine, or add together somehow, to produce an overall motive for acting*. For convenience, call this the "Thesis of Motivational Additivity". To deny the Thesis of Motivational Additivity is to say that there are some circumstances in which one is motivated to do one thing, and motivated to do another, but there is no sense in which one is motivated to do something merely by virtue of the possession of these two

---

[11] The distinction between all-things-considered motivation and prima facie motivation is employed in Donald Davidson, "Intending", in *Essays on Actions and Events* (Oxford: Clarendon Press, 1980), 83–102.

motives. By analogy, we can imagine a thesis of additivity of physical forces, according to which there is such a thing as the force that is acting on an object that is merely the result of combining the various individual forces acting on the object, or we can imagine a contrary view according to which the only forces acting on an object are the separate individual forces pushing it to do various things.

Is someone who is committed to the Thesis of Motivational Additivity thereby committed to denying that the porter who travels to point B has any motive to do so? If so, then Reid has good reasons to think that cases in which agents adopt one of various equivalently good means to their ends are cases in which agents act with no motive at all. In fact, there is some reason to think that the Thesis of Motivational Additivity has this implication. Notice, first, that some ordinary examples would seem to be counter-examples to the Thesis of Motivational Additivity. Imagine that a man has two shillings in his pocket, but believes himself only to have one. His aim is to pay someone a shilling, and he is thereby motivated to pay with shilling #1. He then discovers that shilling #2 is also in his pocket, but still pays with shilling #1. On the discovery, is there any change whatsoever in his motive to pay with shilling #1? Assuming that there really is no difference between the two shillings, and nothing to be gained by paying with one of them rather than another, then there is little reason to think that the discovery of the second shilling dampens, strengthens, or in any other way affects his motivation to pay with shilling #1. But then it seems that the Thesis of Motivational Additivity is shown to be false by this case: the man's motivational attitude towards what he does is unaffected by the addition of other motives for competing actions, and so it seems to follow that those additional motives are not combining with his other motives at all.

However, if we are to hold on to the Thesis of Motivational Additivity even in the face of the considerations just offered against it, we might claim that the case is misdescribed. Perhaps, on the discovery of the second shilling, the man loses his motive to pay with shilling #1, and yet still pays with that shilling. That is, perhaps the man simply acts without a motive. On this model, the discovery of the second shilling creates a counter-balancing motive that places the man in motivational suspense. The discovery of the second shilling does give the man a new motive—a motive to pay with shilling #2; and this new motive combines with the motive to pay with shilling #1. What is the resulting combination? It can't be a motive in favor of paying with shilling #1—why would a motive to do *something else* have that effect? Nor would it be a motive to pay with shilling #2. Nor would it be a motive to do something else entirely—the man still needs to pay a shilling. If there is a motivational state that results from the combining of the motive to pay with the one shilling and the motive to pay with the other, it would seem to be the null motivational state: the state of not being motivated to do either. The man is not motivated, all things considered, to do anything, on this line, because he is equally motivated to do two competing things. Yet, he still pays with shilling #1, and thus acts without any motive at all. To describe the case in this way is to hold on to the Thesis of Motivational Additivity, but to take its consequence to be that people sometimes act without a motive.

Reid seems to accept the Thesis of Motivational Additivity, as illustrated by his discussion of Gregory's example. And he accepts what is, as has just been argued, one of its implications: people sometimes act without any motive at all. But unless the defender of the claim that motives are physical causes must also accept the Thesis of Motivational Additivity, he needn't give up the claim that motives are physical causes. Thus, we are reduced to the following question: is there any reason to think that someone who holds motives to be among the physical causes of action is thereby committed to the Thesis of Motivational Additivity? I don't think there is. Even an adherent to a naturalistic theory of action might draw a distinction between two different roles that motives can play in deliberation. On the one hand, a motive can be considered "a legitimate candidate of satisfaction",[12] and thus prevail or be outweighed by competing considerations; on the other, a motive can be considered an outlaw from deliberation, disallowed even from playing a role on the losing side in the weighing of reasons for and against a particular course of conduct. When a motive plays the first role, it is added together with other motives in accordance with the peculiar calculus involved in the weighing of reasons; but when it plays the second role, it is not added in with the others at all. And yet, even in the second sense, it is one of the agent's motives. If an advocate of the view that motives are among the physical causes of action can allow that a motive should play the second role, then there is no reason to think that such a person must accept the Thesis of Motivational Additivity. But it is hard to see what would preclude an advocate of such a view from holding that an agent can be motivated to do something, even though the motive to do so is granted no deliberative weight. The claim that motives are physical causes,

---

[12] The phrase is Harry Frankfurt's. See his "Identification and Wholeheartedness" in *The Importance of What we Care about* (Cambridge: Cambridge University Press, 1988), 170.

138 · *The Influence of Motives*

that is, doesn't seem to preclude the possibility of denying the Thesis of Motivational Additivity.

While this is a speculative suggestion, it seems nonetheless quite possible that Reid takes cases of agents who act in the face of motivational equilibrium to act with no motive at all because of his acceptance of the Thesis of Motivational Additivity. Further, Newtonian physics encourages the thought that all physical forces are additive, and so encourages those who take the push of motives to be, like physical forces, the push of law, to also accept the Thesis of Motivational Additivity. And, to be sure, a theory of motivation under which that thesis is true is tidier than one that denies it. However, what has been shown in this section is that this is a tidiness in which the defender of the claim that motives are physical causes cannot indulge. To hold on to the claim that motives are physical causes, such a theorist must deny that motives necessarily add together, or push as one.

An Argument from Analogy with Advice

Although Reid is clear in his adamant opposition to the view that the relation between motives and the actions they motivate is anything like the relation either between efficient or physical causes and their respective effects, he is far less clear in his own account of the motive–action relation. There are few places in which Reid can be taken to be offering anything like a positive theory of the influence of motives on behavior. In the few places in which he might be taken to be doing so, he employs a metaphor: the metaphor of advice or persuasion. Sometimes the metaphor is employed in order to capture the influence not of all motives, but only of the rational motives, those that influence our judgments about what ought or ought not to be done. For instance:

[T]hese two principles [that is, passion and reason] influence the will in different ways. Their influence differs, not in degree only, but in kind. This difference we feel, though it may be difficult to find words to express it. We may perhaps more easily form a notion of it by a similitude.

It is one thing to push a man from one part of the room to another; it is a thing of a very different nature to use arguments to persuade him to leave his place, and go to another. (*EAP* II. 2, p. 74/536b)[13]

---

[13] This remark encourages the thought that perhaps Reid's anti-causalism about motivational influence extends only to the influence of rational motives. Perhaps, that is, Reid takes motives that are mediated by a judgment to the effect that something is worth doing to

However, in various places Reid uses the metaphor of advice, or persuasion to describe the influence of every motive, and not just the rational motives. For instance:

[Motives] may be compared to advice, or exhortation, which leaves a man still at liberty.   (*EAP* IV. 4, p. 283/608*b*–609*a*)

Contrary motives may very properly be compared to advocates pleading the opposite sides of a cause at the bar.   (*EAP* IV. 4, p. 288/611*a*)

Given that Reid thinks that "[t]he grand and the important competition of contrary motives is between the animal, on the one hand, and the rational on the other" (*EAP* IV. 4, p. 291/612*a*) he must think that both the animal motives and the rational are like "advocates . . . at the bar".

Be that as it may, it is far from clear what the metaphor of advice, or advocacy, really amounts to. For one thing, it is not so clear that it is not, itself, a causal metaphor. Isn't the advice that someone gives you among the (physical) causes of your following it? And even if advice is understood as bearing a non-causal relation to the act of complying with it, it is still unclear what the advice–action relation is. To analyze one concept, that of the influence of motives, through appeal to another that is just as problematic, the influence of advice, is not to make much progress. But rather than seeing the analogy with advice as intended as a substantive account of the influence of motives on action, it should be taken to have a different purpose. The analogy provides Reid with yet another argument against the view that the influence of motives is a species of physical-causal influence.

The argument from analogy with advice is best seen through consideration of an instructive passage in which Reid enlarges on the analogy between motivational influence and the influence of advice. He writes: "[Motives] may be compared to advice, or exhortation, which leaves a man still at liberty. For in vain is advice given when there is not a power either to do, or to forbear, what it recommends. In like manner, motives suppose liberty in the agent, otherwise they have no influence at all" (*EAP* IV. 4, pp. 283–4/608*b*–609*a*). In this passage, Reid notes a particular feature of

influence action in some non-causal way, while motives that threaten pain, should we act contrary to them, have a causal influence on behavior. While Reid does say things that suggest this—in fact, he never describes anything other than "animal" motives as providing an impulse to action, or as pushing us to act—it is hard to see how such a view could be made consistent with his arguments against the view of motives as either efficient or physical causes. Those arguments seem to apply promiscuously to all motives, and not just to the rational motives for action.

advice, claims that motives have a similar feature, and concludes that motives, like advice, do not influence action in such a way as to undermine liberty. First, consider the feature of advice that is extended, by analogy to motives.

Reid claims that advice is given "in vain" if the person to whom it is given lacks the power to comply with it. There is a sense in which this is true. It doesn't serve any purpose to give advice to a person lacking the power to comply, or, rather, it does not serve the particular distinctive purpose that makes a bit of advice *advice*. The distinctive purpose of advice is to lead its recipient to perform a particular advised action *out of the recognition that the action is worth doing for the reason cited by the advice*. If the recipient of the advice either does not perform the advised action, or performs it for some reason other than that cited in the advice, then the advice has not accomplished its distinctive aim. Conversely, if the aim of the adviser is served just as well by compliant action performed without any recognition of the reason that the advice cites, then the adviser is not offering *true* advice, or advice offered for the sake of the distinctive end served by advice. You might, for instance, offer someone a bit of advice with the same purpose that you have in applying some form of force to the person: in both cases, you might be aiming to get that person to do what you want. But in this case the role that the advice is intended to play could, perhaps, be played just as easily by a lie, a threat, or even a shove. In such cases, advice is not being used in its characteristic manner; it is not serving its constitutive aim. So when Reid says that advice is given in vain to those who lack the power to comply with it, he must mean that advice cannot serve its *distinctive purpose* if given to someone who lacks the power to comply with it.

Reid's contention that the distinctive purpose of advice presupposes power, in his sense, on the part of the person to whom the advice is given is not clearly true. In order to accomplish the distinctive aim of advice, the person to whom it is given must be capable of acting on a particular reason, namely the reason cited by the adviser. But only if acting on a reason requires active power will it follow from this that advice presupposes power on the part of the person to whom it is issued. No one who accepts a theory of action under which action is possible without the possession of active power will agree to this conclusion, for the capacity to act on reasons is among those capacities that any satisfactory theory of action must model. A naturalistic theory of agency, then, will claim that to act on reasons is to be physically caused to act, and will go on to specify what physical-causal history an act must have for it to count as action on a reason; it will specify, that is, what laws must be instantiated by a bit of behavior for that behavior to count as action-for-a-reason. As we will see, Reid doesn't have to be right in claiming that the distinctive purpose of advice presupposes active power for his argument from analogy with advice to succeed.

Reid claims, also, that advice is given in vain to someone who lacks the power *not* to comply with the advice. It is not surprising that Reid should hold this, given that he thinks that possession of the power to act entails possession of the power not to act (a point discussed in Chapter 2): if advice is given in vain in the absence of the power to comply with it, and if a person has the power to comply with it only if he also has the power not to comply with it, then advice is given in vain in the absence of the power not to comply with it.[14]

But even if these results about advice are correct—namely, that advice fails to accomplish its distinctive purpose if its recipient lacks either the power to comply with it or the power not to—what do they tell us about the influence of motives? In the passage under consideration, Reid claims that motives are like advice since they "suppose liberty in the agent, otherwise they have no influence at all". It is far from clear what, exactly, this means. It makes some sense to say that advice can "have no influence at all" in the absence of liberty on the part of the person who receives it; at least,

---

[14] One natural reason to think that advice presupposes the power not to comply with it cannot be accepted by Reid. We might think this is true because we think that there is no point in trying to get someone to act some way if it's inevitable that he is going to act that way; in such a case, why waste the effort? This, coupled with the claim that to give advice is always to try to get someone to do something, seems to lead to the conclusion that there's no point in giving advice to someone who lacks the power not to comply with it. However, this result does not, in fact, follow, despite appearances. A person could fail to perform a particular act while lacking the power not to perform that act; the failure could be something caused by another agent entirely, and not by the person who fails. This is true under the analysis that Reid must accept of Locke's example discussed in Ch. 2. There it was argued that Reid must hold that a man in a locked room who chooses to stay in the room lacks the power to leave *and* the power to stay. So, although the man fails to leave the room, his failure to do so is not a product of his active power, and so is no true action of his. Accordingly, in the absence of independent reasons to think that the power to act entails the power to refrain from acting, there might be good reason to advise a person to perform a particular act even if that person lacks the power not to perform that act. Say, for instance, that you know that the man in the locked room will injure himself if he tries to leave, but you don't want to inform him that he's locked in. You might then advise him to stay, and perhaps, thereby, prompt his staying, even though he lacks the power to leave. So, unless we already accept that the power to act entails the power to refrain from action, there is no reason to think that the distinctive function of advice could not be served even if it's recipient lacks the power to act contrary to it.

142 · *The Influence of Motives*

it makes sense to say that advice cannot have its *distinctive* influence, the influence that leads someone to act as it dictates for the reason that it specifies, in the absence of liberty on the part of the recipient of the advice. But without some specification of the distinctive purpose of motives—a specification, that is, of what the constitutive aim of a motive is—it is hard to see what the comparable claim about motives really amounts to. In order for the analogy to work, Reid must think that there is some end towards which motives tend by virtue of which they count as *motives*, and not as mere pushes or impulses.

Before turning to the question of whether or not motives have some constitutive end, and, if so, what that end might be, it is helpful to have in hand a schematic account of the argument under discussion. Reid can be taken to be offering the following argument for the claim that advice does not have a physical-causal influence:

(6a) If S's A-ing is physically caused, then S does not have the power to A.

(6b) If in A-ing S is following someone's advice (that is, if the advice to A is serving its characteristic purpose), then S has the power to A.

∴ (6c) If in A-ing S is following someone's advice, then S's A-ing is not physically caused.

∴ The influence of advice is not a form of physical-causal influence.

In claiming that there is an analogy between the influence of motives and the influence of advice, Reid is offering an argument to the conclusion that motives do not have a physical-causal influence that can be constructed by paraphrasing (6a), (6b), and (6c) so that they concern the influence of motives, rather than the influence of advice. The resulting argument is the following:

(6.1) If S's A-ing is physically caused, then S does not have the power to A.

(6.2) If S's A-ing is motivated (that is, if in A-ing S's motive to A is serving its characteristic purpose), then S has the power to A.

∴ (6.3) If S's A-ing is motivated, then S's A-ing is not physically caused.

∴ Motivational influence is not a form of physical-causal influence.

The central idea of the argument is very simple. If a motive can influence only someone who has power to act as it directs, and if a motive's having physical-causal influence would undermine that power, then motives can have influence only if their influence is not like the influence of ordinary physical causes.

The driving force of this argument is premise (6.2). However, the argument also depends on the metaphysics of power discussed in earlier chapters. Premise (6.1), for instance, depends on both the claim that an event that is physically caused is efficiently caused by the creature whose resolution accounts for the truth of the relevant law, and the claim that no event can have more than one efficient cause.[15] Even given these two claims, it does not strictly follow that the physical causation of action by motivation is incompatible with power on the part of the agent. However, it fails to follow only under those conditions in which a motive physically causes behavior in accordance with a law authored by the agent himself. As noted earlier, since Reid is primarily concerned to rebut naturalistic conceptions of human action, he would not be threatened by this possibility. Still, the crucial point is that premise (6.1) could be rejected by rejecting the various claims about the nature of power on which it rests.

Is premise (6.2) true? One question to ask about it is this: what reasons are there to believe that motives have any characteristic purpose at all? Advice has a characteristic purpose for conceptual reasons. It is part of the concept of advice that the adviser aims to accomplish a particular task, and it is that task that differentiates advising from other related acts such as deceiving, coercing, cajoling, or seducing. But can a comparable claim be made about motives? Is there any reason to think that motives are to be distinguished from other moving forces, such as pushes and pulls, by appeal to some characteristic purpose? Maybe they have no such purpose at all.

Because of his theistic commitments, Reid assumes that every feature of the world serves a distinctive purpose. However, it is one thing to hold that there is some good reason why people are motivated to do what they do, rather than, say, programmed, and quite another to hold that it is in the nature of motivation to serve that purpose. To make the latter claim is to believe that the concept of motivation is teleological—that a world in which motives are not given to serve their peculiar end is a world that lacks motives, strictly speaking, entirely. There are, arguably anyway, some things that the world would not include were they not purposeful in a particular way. Were the bits of paper and metal that we call "money" suddenly to be granted no role in the exchange of goods and services, it is arguable that they would stop being money; to be of use in this manner, or

---

[15] This latter claim was named the principle of Efficient-Causal Exclusivity in Ch. 2.

at least to aim at being of use in this manner, is definitive of what it is to be money. Are motives like that?

The question is different from the analogous question about money, or advice, because motives are purposes—they are that for the sake of which we act. So, what is being asked is whether the having of purposes has a characteristic purpose. While it can't be considered as an argument for the claim that motives do, indeed, have a characteristic purpose, Reid does make a point that gives some support to that claim. He writes:

[N]ature intended that we should be active, and we need some principle to incite us to action, when we happen not to be invited by any appetite or passion.

For this end, when strength and spirits are recruited by rest, nature has made total inaction as uneasy as excessive labour.

We may call this the principle of *activity*. It is most conspicuous in children, who cannot be supposed to know how useful and necessary it is for their improvement to be constantly employed. Their constant activity therefore appears not to proceed from their having some end constantly in view, but rather from this, that they desire to be always doing something, and feel uneasiness in total inaction. (*EAP* III. 2. i, pp. 123–4/553a–b)

The having of an end, any end, has instrumental value: it serves as a means to the end of *doing* something. Reid adds that "nature intended" that we should be doing something, rather than nothing; this is his way of saying that the purpose of having ends, or being motivated, is characteristic of motivation. While Reid offers little by way of proof that nature intended motives for that purpose—although he does cite the misery of those who do nothing—there is surely something right about the idea. There are goods to be had by aiming towards ends that cannot be had any other way, and this fact suggests that the tendency to produce those goods is the characteristic function of motivation.

Say we accept that motives have some characteristic purpose—that a particular item in the etiology of action is not a motive if it is not possessed for the sake of some distinctive purpose—then there is an obvious further question to answer: what is the point of being motivated, rather than merely being pushed about? The point can't be that without motives we wouldn't move around the world or complete ordinary tasks. Wind-up toys move about, and we can imagine robots that eat, reproduce, paint pictures, express opinions, and call meetings to order. Motivation simply isn't essential for the production of the everyday behaviors in which we engage. Another way to put the question: if you were assigned the task of creating the universe and populating it with creatures, for what purpose would you find it necessary to give some of those creatures motives? What would you want the world to include that would be left out were nothing motivated to act?

Reid holds that there is a certain value instantiated by end-directed behavior that is missing from qualitatively identical behavior that is not similarly end-directed. He describes the view that only motivated behavior can have "merit or demerit" as "a self-evident proposition" (*EAP* IV. 4, pp. 286/609*b*–610*a*). In addition, and relatedly, in various places he suggests that morally assessible behavior is behavior for which an "account" needs to be given (cf. *EIP* VI. 5, p. 628). To give an account of one's behavior is to specify the relation that one takes that behavior to bear to one's ends. A bit of behavior that is neither performed for its own sake, nor as a means to some other end, cannot be subsumed under a more general principle that the agent aims to instantiate in his conduct; it cannot be placed in the order of reasons. But it is the placement in such an order—it is the "account" that can be offered for an act—that gives that act its moral value or disvalue. Were there no end-directed behavior, that is, there would be no morally valuable behavior.

The idea that the value of an act derives entirely from the value of the end at which the act is aimed is an idea developed in various ways in eighteenth-century philosophy. It is the motivating idea behind Kant's famous claim that the only thing good in itself is a good will.[16] If the will is understood as the capacity to direct one's conduct towards an end, then to claim that only the good will is good in itself is to claim that whatever value attaches to an act derives from the end at which the act is aimed; if that end is good, so is the act. The idea is developed also (to give just one other example) by Shaftesbury. He writes:

[T]he beautiful, the fair, the comely, were never in the matter, but in the art and design, never in body itself, but in the form or forming power. Does not the beautiful form confess this, and speak the beauty of the design whenever it strikes you? What is it but the design which strikes? What is it you admire but mind, or the effects of mind? It

---

[16] For instance: "A good will is not good because of what it effects or accomplishes, because of its fitness to attain some proposed end, but only because of its volition, that is, it is good in itself and, regarded for itself, is to be valued incomparably higher than all that could merely be brought about by it in favor of some inclination and indeed, if you will, of the sum of all inclinations" (Immanuel Kant, "Groundwork of the Metaphysics of Morals", in *Practical Philosophy: The Cambridge Edition of the Works of Immanuel Kant*, tr. and ed. M. J. Gregor (Cambridge: Cambridge University Press, 1996), 50).

is mind alone which forms. All which is void of mind is horrid, and matter formless is deformity itself.[17]

Behind everything beautiful must be a mind that designed the parts to be related to each other as they are. Without such a mind, a legislator of the pattern in which the parts sit, we have nothing but an accidental conglomerate. The reason that the designed collection of separate entities is of value is that it indicates the presence in the world of the truly valuable thing: namely, the "design" or "form", the instantiation of which is the point, or purpose, of the conglomerate. There would be no value in an object or an act, Shaftesbury thinks, if there were no end at which the object or act aimed.

For Reid, as for many other philosophers of his period, a world in which no one was motivated to act, a world, that is, in which nothing was directed towards ends, would be a world absent of genuine moral (and aesthetic) value or disvalue. A motive, then, can be thought of as a kind of invitation: an invitation to instantiate in one's conduct the particular degree of moral value or disvalue possessed by an act performed for the sake of the end specified by the motive. If we add the further claim that whatever value an act has can be attributed only to the efficient cause of the act—a view that Reid also holds (cf. *EIP* VI. 6, p. 478)—then the analogy between motives and advice starts to come into focus. Advice cannot serve its characteristic aim of inducing its recipient to perform an act for the reason the advice specifies unless the recipient of the advice has the power to perform the act; similarly, motives cannot serve their characteristic aim of inducing their possessor to perform an act that instantiates moral value or disvalue unless the motivated agent has the power to perform the act specified by the motive. What advice and motives have in common is this: a necessary condition for each to accomplish its characteristic aim is the possession of power by the agent to which they are applied.

A moment ago, I asked a question: what good thing would the world necessarily lack if no one were motivated to act? I then moved into discussion of what good thing the world would necessarily lack if there were no end-directed behavior. The answer was anything of either moral or aesthetic value. But, even if this is true, the point only serves Reid's aims if it is not possible for there to be end-directed behavior without motivation. In fact, this claim can be questioned. We might think that it is possible for

[17] Shaftesbury, "The Moralists: A Philosophical Rhapsody", in *Characteristicks of Men, Manners, Opinions, Times*, ed. Lawrence Klein (Cambridge: Cambridge University Press, 1999), 322.

a creature, an organism, to be end-directed in its behavior without having any thought about the end at which it aims. We might think, for instance, that the jellyfish really does aim to kill that fish and eat it, but to imagine that the jellyfish has in its mind a thought about that result that plays a role in the etiology of its behavior is to attribute the jellyfish with one thought more than it has ever had. If it is possible to naturalize teleology without appeal to the natural role of mental representations of the ends at which behavior is aimed, then it is possible to build end-directedness into the universe without giving anything a motive to act.[18] Still, the instantiation of moral or aesthetic value probably does require end-directedness deriving from some representation of, or thought about, the end in question on the part of the creature given credit or blame for bringing about something with the relevant form of value. Whatever attraction this thought has probably comes from the recognition of some kind of constitutive link between responsibility and self-consciousness of one's own responsibility. Perhaps for behavior to be end-directed is not necessarily for it to be thought about; but for one to be the author of the relevant valuable or disvaluable thing requires that one think about the end from which that thing's value derives.

We are now in position to return to the question of how Reid distinguishes between motivated animal behavior—which he takes to be physically caused by motives—and motivated human behavior. Since the analogy with advice extends not just to the rational motives but to the animal as well, it might appear that Reid is committed to the claim that when an animal acts on a motive it, too, is responding in a way analogous to the way in which people respond to advice. If in the case of human beings the distinctive purpose of a motive precludes the possibility that the motive is having a physical-causal influence, then it might appear that the same is true of animal behavior, thus implying that animals are not, in fact, physically caused to act by their motives. This point could be put as a challenging question: why doesn't Reid's argument from analogy with advice show him to be wrong in his contention that animal behavior is physically caused by motives?

[18] For some recent discussion of the prospects for a naturalistic account of teleology cf. Larry Wright, *Teleological Explanations: An Etiological Analysis of Goals and Functions* (Los Angeles: University of California Press, 1976); Andrew Woodfield, *Teleology* (Cambridge: Cambridge University Press, 1976); T. L. Short, "Teleology in Nature", *American Philosophical Quarterly*, 20/4 (Oct. 1983), 311–20; Nancy Cartwright, "Two Kinds of Teleological Explanation", in A. N. Perovich and M. V. Wedin (eds.), *Human Nature and Natural Knowledge* (Dordrecht: Reidel Publishing, 1986); William Fitzpatrick, *Teleology and the Norms of Nature* (New York: Garland Press, 2000).

However, the question can be answered. Since animals are incapable of instantiating moral value or disvalue in their conduct, the distinctive purpose of motivation in animals is not the same as the distinctive purpose of human motivation. The purpose of motivation in animals—the reason that animals are motivated to act as they do rather than merely programmed—is biological survival. Their uneasinesses—which are the only kind of motivation they have—point them away, in general, from those things that will interfere with their survival, and point them towards those things essential for it. But this distinctive purpose does not require the power, in Reid's sense, to act as directed by the relevant motives. The analogy with advice breaks down, that is, when we are discussing the motives of animals. What follows is that animal behavior is not, for Reid, end-directed behavior. Animal behavior does serve an end—the animal's survival—but that end is set by the author of the laws linking animal behavior with motives and not by the animal itself. Strictly speaking, then, animal behavior is not motivated behavior even though motives play a (physical-causal) role in its etiology. Reid accepts the following conditional: if a bit of behavior is genuinely end-directed, then it is not physically caused. With respect to human behavior he affirms the antecedent; with respect to animal behavior he denies the consequent.

The argument from analogy with advice, then, rests on something like the following reasoning. The point of being motivated, as human beings are, is to instantiate moral value in one's conduct; conduct that is not self-consciously end-directed has no moral value or disvalue. But since conduct is not morally valuable or disvaluable, Reid thinks, if it is not efficiently caused by the agent who is to be attributed with the conduct's moral value or disvalue, it follows that motivation cannot accomplish its characteristic purpose unless the conduct that it motivates is efficiently caused by the motivated agent. Just as the point of advising someone, rather than, say, coercing him, is to get him to do something through his own power, the point of being motivated, rather than, say, pushed, is to prompt him to act under his own power.

Conclusion

While none of Reid's arguments against naturalistic conceptions of human agency—views according to which the push of motives is the push of law—are decisive, they are highly suggestive and amount to the identification of difficult tasks that a naturalist about human agency would have to perform to provide an adequate defense of his view. The first argument shows not that there are no laws linking our motives with our conduct, but, instead, that whatever optimism one might have that there are such laws cannot be derived from the seeming truth of the claim that people act on their strongest motive. It is too easy, and too tempting, to employ a trivial notion of strength of motivation. Under any non-trivial account, difficult empirical work that cannot be done from the armchair is required to determine if we always act on our strongest motive.

The second argument also poses a difficult task for the defender of the claim that motives are physical causes. With limitations, we understand well enough how physical forces combine so as to influence the behavior of the objects on which they act. But if we accept that motivational forces are additive, then it would seem that we must deny that human beings are always motivated to act, and so must deny that every action has motives among its physical causes. While a more sophisticated view of motivation that allows for the possibility of motives that push, but do not combine with other motives the agent has, is not obviously, or necessarily, inconsistent with the view that motives are physical causes, further work is required to see whether or not the analogy between motivational forces and natural forces breaks down if we allow that motives are not necessarily additive.

The argument from the analogy with advice presents a challenge to naturalistic models of human agency of an entirely different sort. Naturalists must allow that there are some concepts—such as the concept of advice—under which particulars fall only if they are aimed in a certain way. If the concept of motivation is of this sort, and if Reid is right that an influence on action counts as a motive only if it aims towards the production of end-directed behavior uniquely capable of instantiating distinctive forms of value, then the third of Reid's arguments against the view that motives are physical causes can be rejected only through the wholesale rejection of Reid's metaphysics of power and exertion. While Reid's conception of power, exertion, and natural change may very well be problematic, what the argument from the analogy with advice shows is that it is only a short step from it to an anti-causalist view of motivation. In short, then, all of Reid's arguments illustrate that a satisfactory version of a theory under which the influence of motives is reducible to the influence of natural laws must be sophisticated indeed.

Conclusion: Agent Causation and the Regress of Effort

In the introduction to this book, a distinction was drawn between two different ways in which one might think about teleological explanations: one might think of them as appealing, ultimately, to basic, irreducible qualities of end-directedness to be found throughout nature, even in unconscious chunks of stuff—qualities like "dormitive virtues" or "substantial forms"—or one might think of them as appealing, ultimately, to basic, irreducible intentions of agents, qualities that can be found only in creatures with minds. Anyone who holds, as Reid does, that physical causation occurs by virtue of the fact that agents act for the sake of achieving certain ends must also hold that the basic qualities appealed to in teleological explanations, however construed, direct objects towards ends without doing so by virtue of their physical-causal functioning. In compliance with the Baconian and Newtonian tradition, Reid eschews teleology that involves attributing mindless objects with basic qualities of end-directedness. However, he holds that all change to be found is ultimately teleological in the second sense: wherever there is change there is an agent with the intention to enact that change. Further, human beings have a prerogative otherwise reserved only for God and angels: we are the agents of many of the changes to be found; they come about to further our ends.

Having seen Reid's grounds for holding this view, we are now in position to see how Reid's position relates to contemporary agent-causalism. According to the agent-causal position (represented in the work of Roderick Chisholm, Richard Taylor, Timothy O'Connor, and Randolph Clarke, among others[1]),

---

[1] Cf. Roderick Chisholm, "Human Freedom and the Self", in G. Watson (ed.) *Free Will* Oxford: Oxford University Press, 1982, 24–35; Richard Taylor, *Action and Purpose* (Englewood Cliffs, NJ: Prentice-Hall, 1966); Randolph Clarke, "Toward a Credible Agent-Causal Account of

free actions are caused by agents or persons and not merely by events taking place in the mind and body of the agent. Thus, according to agent-causalists, facts aptly described with causal verbs and agents as subject are not necessarily reducible to facts aptly described with causal verbs and events and states as subjects; any fact that is reducible to the causal functioning of events and states is not a fact about the free action of an agent. Agent-causalists hold that there is a relation that holds between an agent and an action when the action is free that is both basic and causal. The relation is basic in the sense that its obtaining between an agent and an action does not simply amount to, or supervene on, the obtaining of other independent relations. However, it is more difficult to say exactly what is meant in claiming that a relation is causal. Agent-causalists often point out that it is no easier for someone who denies the possibility of agent causation to say what it is about the relation between events—the relation between, say, the movement of the ball and the breaking of the window—that makes that relation a causal one. Without begging the question against the agent-causalist, one can't deny that a basic causal relation can obtain between an agent and an action on the grounds that no relation between these relata would be causal.

Reid is often described as an agent-causalist.[2] But it is a bit unclear if this is correct. Reid does say things that sound like statements of agent-causalism. For instance, "I grant . . . that an effect uncaused is a contradiction, and that an event uncaused is an absurdity. The question that remains is whether a volition, undetermined by motives, is an event uncaused. This I deny. The cause of the volition is the man who willed it" (*COR* 123, p. 234; see also *EAP* IV. 4, p. 288/610*b*). Shortly after this remark, Reid makes it clear that when he says that the "cause of the volition is the man who willed it" he is using the term "cause" in the sense of efficient causality. It is true that Reid thinks that only agents are efficient causes; no event or state could be an efficient cause, because an event or state is not the sort of thing that can have a power and exert it. This suggests that the very definition of efficient causation imports agent-causalism: if a philosopher believes that there is

Free Will", in T. O'Connor (ed.), *Agents, Causes and Events: Essays on Indeterminism and Free Will* (New York: Oxford University Press, 1995), 201–15; Timothy O'Connor, "Agent Causation", in T. O'Connor (ed.), *Agents, Causes and Events: Essays on Indeterminism and Free Will* (New York: Oxford University Press, 1995), 173–200.

[2] Cf. William Rowe, *Thomas Reid on Freedom and Morality* (Ithaca, NY: Cornell University Press 1991); Timothy O'Connor, "Thomas Reid on Free Agency", *Journal for the History of Philosophy*, 32/4, (1994), 605–22; Keith Lehrer, *Thomas Reid* (London: Routledge, 1989).

efficient causation, in Reid's sense, one might think, then he is an agent-causalist. This is too quick, however. Efficient causality amounts to agent causalism only if the relation "efficient causes" is basic, or else obtains only if some other basic causal relation obtains. But is this so, under Reid's definition of efficient causation? The efficient causal relation obtains between an agent and an event by virtue of the obtaining of three relations: (1) a relation between the agent and his power, (2) a relation between the agent and his exertion of power, and (3) a relation between, on the one hand, power and exertion, and, on the other, the relevant event. Unless one of these three relations is a basic causal relation, or obtains only if some other basic causal relation obtains, the efficient causal relation seems to admit of reduction. Further, it is not immediately obvious that any of the three relations to which it reduces are basic causal relations between an agent and an event. The relation between the agent and his power is just the same as the relation between any object and its properties. The relation between the power–exertion pair and the event that is efficiently caused is a relation that takes only events, states, and properties as relata. So, if there is a case to be made that Reid is an agent-causalist, it would seem to rest on the claim that to appeal to the relation between the agent and his exertion of power is to appeal to a basic causal relation, either because that relation is, itself, a basic causal relation or, perhaps, because the exertion itself is a basic causal relation between an agent and an event.

It is striking that, in the passage just quoted, it is in characterizing the relation between the agent and his volition that Reid is most naturally taken to be making a statement of agent-causalism. As we've learnt, all volitions for Reid are exertions of power to act, so this is strong evidence that Reid thinks of the agent–exertion relation as a causal relation. It is odd, however, that Reid should characterize that relation as the relation of efficient causation. If he is to be consistent in his notion of efficient causation, then he must hold that agents are the efficient causes of their volitions, their exertions, in virtue of having the power to exert and exerting that power. As we've seen, Reid does think that any agent who has the power to act in a certain way also has the power to exert that power. But is the power to exert exercised through exertion? If so, then regress looms. If the relation between the agent and his exertion is to be analyzed in the same way as the relation between the agent and the effect that he exerts himself to produce, then the relation between the agent and his exertion obtains in part by virtue of a relation between the agent and his exertion of his power to exert; that relation, in turn, obtains by virtue in part of a relation between the agent and his exertion of his power to exert his power to exert; and so on.

Exactly how Reid understands the relations involved in efficient causation has been examined closely in the recent secondary literature on Reid. In this connection, a dispute has arisen regarding Reid's view of the nature of exertions of power. William Rowe takes exertions of power to be events; they are causings of the events that follow from them. Although he thinks it likely that so understood exertions would not meet Reid's criteria for an event, he takes them to be events in the sense in which the term is used in contemporary philosophical discussion.[3] Timothy O'Connor, by contrast, thinks that for Reid an exertion is, itself, a *relation* that holds between an agent and event if and only if the agent causes the event.[4] For both Rowe and O'Connor, however, exertions of power are not occurrences that the agent must bring about in order to bring about something else, but are, instead, *the bringing about* of that that the agent is exerting himself to produce.[5] So, according to both Rowe and O'Connor, the efficient causal relation holds only if a basic causal relation between an agent and an event holds. The exertion, on Rowe's view, is what constitutes the basic causal relation between the agent and the event of which he is the efficient cause; on O'Connor's view, the exertion just is that basic causal relation. Under either interpretation, the fact that an agent is the efficient cause of an event only if he has the power to bring the event about and exerts that power does not undermine the claim that Reid is an agent causalist. Ultimately, for both Rowe and O'Connor, the efficient causal relation obtains only if some basic causal relation between an agent and event obtains also.

Rowe and O'Connor are both concerned to rescue Reid from the problems of regress that would seem to plague his view given the definition of efficient causation. In order to do so, they both hold that, whatever relation obtains between the agent and his exertion of power, it is not the relation

[3] See, for instance, Rowe, *Reid on Freedom and Morality*, 153–8, and Rowe, "The Metaphysics of Freedom: Reid's Theory of Agent Causation", *American Catholic Philosophical Quarterly*, 74/3, (2000), 425–46 (esp. pp. 438–46).

[4] See Timothy O'Connor, "Thomas Reid on Free Agency", *Journal for the History of Philosophy*, 32/4, (1994), 605–22 (esp. p. 620) and O'Connor, *Persons and Causes: The Metaphysics of Free Will* (New York: Oxford University Press, 2000), esp. p. 47.

[5] Both Rowe and O'Connor, however, think that the coming to be of exertion, however exertion is understood, is something uncaused (cf. Rowe, *Reid on Freedom and Morality*, 154, and O'Connor, "Reid on Free Agency", 621). Rowe and O'Connor take different steps, the details of which are not important for our purposes, to explain why this fact does not impugn Reid's acceptance of the claim that every event is efficiently caused, and why it does not undermine the agent's responsibility for his exertion of power.

of efficient causality, under Reid's official definition of the term. Under both of their interpretations, the agent is not the efficient cause of his exertion of power any more than an event is the physical cause of the causal relation holding between itself and its physical effects. Since Reid explicitly says that the agent is the efficient cause of his volition, and since he is committed to the view that all exertions of power are volitions, both Rowe and O'Connor paint Reid as inconsistent in his usage of the term "efficient cause". It would be remarkable if Reid were inconsistent in this way, given how persnickety he is about the usage of the term. Of course, this doesn't imply that he was not inconsistent in his usage of the term, but only that an interpretation under which the relation between the agent and his exertions of power is the relation of efficient causation would be a more charitable and hence superior interpretation. The question is whether it is possible to provide such an interpretation without falling prey to problems of regress.

The solution to the problem emerges when one thinks about the notion of "trying". If an agent tries to do something and succeeds in doing it, he did only one thing; it would be wrong to say that he did two things, try and succeed. We don't, for instance, prosecute the successful murderer for both murder and attempted murder and then make him serve consecutive sentences. If he committed the murder, then his attempt to do so wasn't a separate action. However, if an agent tries and fails, he still did something, namely try. Where does the act of trying go in the case of success? One might think that since there must be something in common between the case of success and the case of failure, and since the case of failure involves the performance of the act of trying, it follows, contrary to intuition regarding the term "try", that in the case of success the agent does, in fact, do two things. Someone who takes this position, then, is committed to saying that it is not the metaphysics of agency that makes it inappropriate to prosecute the murderer for attempted murder, in addition to murder—after all the murderer did, under this view, commit at least two acts in violation of the law—but other factors instead. Perhaps, for instance, it would clog the courts to prosecute the murderer for attempted murder; we might, for instance, also need to prosecute him for attempted attempted murder, and for attempted attempted attempted murder, and so on. That's too many cases to prosecute. However, a conclusion of this sort would be odious to Reid. Consider the following passage:

A philosopher is, no doubt, entitled to examine even those distinctions that are to be found in the structure of all languages; and, if he is able to shew that there is no foundation for them in the nature of the things distinguished; if he can point out some predjudice common to mankind which has led them to distinguish things which are not really different; in that case, such a distinction may be imputed to a vulgar error, which ought to be corrected in philosophy. But when, in the first setting out, he takes it for granted without proof, that distinctions found in the structure of all languages, have no foundation in nature; this surely is too fastidious a way of treating the common sense of mankind. (*EIP* I. 1, pp. 26–7)

Reid's claim is that, where we find a well-entrenched linguistic or conceptual fact, we ought to assert that there is to be found a "foundation" for it in nature, until we are shown a reason to think that it is *merely* a fact about our concepts or the language we use to express them. The manifest is, defeasibly, the best guide to the metaphysical. The fact that we don't understand how there could be something in the world that, like trying, is action in the case of failure, but is more than nothing and yet less than action in the case of success, shows only that there are limits to our understanding of the metaphysics, not that there is no such thing to be found. Since the notion of "trying" is deeply embedded in our conceptual and linguistic practices, and since there is no ordinary, non-metaphysical reason to think us mistaken to use it, it must have some "foundation" in nature. There must be something that is involved in every successful voluntary act, and that has some ontological status different from that of ordinary events like actions, and yet rises to the status of action in the case of failure.

There is some evidence to suggest that Reid thought about the grammar of "trying" and noticed precisely the point on which emphasis is being placed here, namely, that in cases of success the attempt is subsumed into the act the agent performs, even though, in cases of failure, the attempt is an action in its own right. He writes: "I will to walk for half an hour. The exertion immediately succeeds. During my walk, my thought is wholly occupied, on some other subject than the walk, so that there is not a thought of it or will concerning it at present in my mind; yet the exertion of walking continues" (OP 5). During the course of the walk, the agent is not willing to walk or consciously trying to walk. Yet the act of walking continues and is the agent's act in the proper sense. Hence it must be something of which the agent is the efficient cause. Thus, we seem to have grounds both for saying that the agent is not exerting himself to walk and that he is exerting himself to walk. In the case of success, the exertion is present, but it is not action; it is not the sort of thing that it is prior to success, or in cases of failure.

Notice, and here is the important point, if exertion is understood as no different from effort, or trying, then there is no regress, and the relation between the agent and his exertion of power—in the only case, namely that of failure, in which the exertion is anything at all—is the relation of efficient causation. If an agent succeeds in acting, then his exertion is no action; it is not something he did or, what's the same, something he efficiently caused. However, if he fails, then his exertion is his act; he is the efficient cause of it. Since, when he fails, he successfully exerted himself, his exertion to exert, in this case, is not some further action of which he is the cause. Exertion, in the case of success, is not action, and so is not something for which an efficient cause must be identified.

The point may seem clearer when expressed in the language of trying, rather than exertion. It is true that you can't do anything unless you try. Does it follow that in order to do something you have to try to try? No, although, arguably anyway, if you fail to act but can be said to try, then you must have tried to try; after all, in that case, what you did was to try, and since you can't do anything unless you try, you must have tried to try. But this doesn't imply that when you succeed you also try to try. In that case, trying was not something that you did; all you did was act. To think there is a regress here is to fail to respect the grammar of "trying", or "exertion".

So what is exertion? What is it to try? The only answer is, it depends whether we are talking about cases of success or cases of failure. In cases of failure, it is action of which the agent is the efficient cause. In cases of success, it is not action. But what is exertion in cases of success? The best answer is: who knows? In such cases the exertion goes where the attempted murder went in the case of a successful murder. It is not part of the metaphysics in such cases; it is not something distinct in the world. If it is anything at all, it is just the action that the agent succeeds in performing, the murder, say, or the bodily movement. If this seems peculiar, which it undeniably does, then all that can be said is that our language tells us that the world is a peculiar place.

So is Reid an agent-causalist? Rowe and O'Connor make the case for thinking that Reid is committed to the existence of a basic causal relation between agents and events on the grounds that without appeal to such a relation his view encounters insoluble problems of regress. I've solved the regress problem in a different way, by drawing on Reid's methodological commitment to the view that the best metaphysics mirrors entrenched linguistic practice, on the grammar of "trying", and on a plausible equation between exertion and trying. Does this commit Reid to belief in the existence of a basic causal relation between agents and events? The answer is yes, but for very different reasons from those advocated by Rowe or O'Connor. Someone who succeeds in doing something did try to do it, it's just that his trying to do it was not a separate action distinct from his doing it. So, whatever relation holds between him and his trying is at most the relation that holds between him and his action; after all, if the trying is anywhere in cases of success it is "in" the successful action.

The question, then, of whether or not Reid is committed to the existence of a basic causal relation between agents and events reduces to the question of whether or not the relation between the agent and the events of which he is the successful efficient cause is a basic causal relation. The case for thinking it is not rests on the following grounds: the efficient causal relation obtains in virtue of the obtaining of relations between the agent and his power, the agent and his exertion, and the power–exertion pair and the effect. However, if, in cases of success, the relation between the agent and the exertion just is the relation between the agent and the effect, then it would follow that in such cases one of the necessary conditions of the agent's standing in the efficient causal relation to the effect is that the agent stands in that relation to the effect. This is hardly a reduction of one relation to others but seems, instead, to be the mark of a relation that cannot be reduced: to explicate what it is for an agent to stand in the efficient causal relation to an effect we need to invoke that very relation. In the only sense in which we are able to conceptualize it, then, the efficient causal relation is a basic causal relation, and it is a relation between an agent and an event.

So, Reid is an agent-causalist but not because he has a well-developed conception of the metaphysics of power—a conception under which an exertion is a causing, or a conception under which an exertion is a relation between agent and effect—but, instead, because he is able to tolerate the mysterious metaphysics that our linguistic practices imply and which bar us from analyzing the efficient causal relation in any way which could count as a reduction. All we are able to know about exertion is what paltry scraps we can deduce from the language of "trying". From that we are able to see that we are flatly incapable of anything that we could recognize as a reduction of the notion of efficient causality. When we succeed, our powers manifest themselves in the actions of which we are the efficient causes. When we fail, the only actions with respect to which we have succeeded are exertions themselves.

Reid, we might say, is a contented mysterianist in at least two important respects. He holds that the efficient causal relation itself is, ultimately, something of which we can have no explanatory grasp, for we are simply incapable of understanding how there could be something like exertion, and yet our language tells us that there must be. Also, he holds that the ubiquitous regularity in the exertion of power—regularity that undergirds both our inductive inferences and our attributions of character traits—is itself the product of resolutions the nature and functioning of which are beyond intelligibility. Both forms of mysterianism, as I hope to have demonstrated, are intertwined with Reid's fundamentally teleological conception of change and of motivated human action. The end-directedness of events and behaviors derives from the mind's capability to direct events towards ends; but how the mind does this in individual cases, and why it does it consistently and regularly, thereby manifesting character traits, are both questions the answers to which are necessarily beyond our grasp. We know how it is, but simply cannot know how it could be that way. Our activity is manifest, and demonstrably different from the ordinary progress of nature.

Bibliography

Adams, Todd (1988) "Motives and Causes in the Scottish Commonsense Tradition", in P. H. Hare (ed.), *Doing Philosophy Historically* (Buffalo, NY: Prometheus Publishing), 283–90.

Bramhall, John (1999) "A Defense of True Liberty", in V. Chappell (ed.) *Hobbes and Bramhall on Liberty and Necessity* (Cambridge: Cambridge University Press).

Cartwright, Nancy (1986) "Two Kinds of Teleological Explanation", in A. N. Perovich and M. V. Wedin (eds.), *Human Nature and Natural Knowledge* (Dordrecht: Reidel Publishing).

Chisholm, Roderick (1982) "Human Freedom and the Self", in G. Watson (ed.), *Free Will* (Oxford: Oxford University Press), 24–35.

Clarke, Randolph (1995) "Toward a Credible Agent-Causal Account of Free Will", in T. O'Connor (ed.), *Agents, Causes and Events: Essays on Indeterminism and Free Will* (New York: Oxford University Press), 201–15.

Clarke, Samuel (1978) *Samuel Clarke, the Works* (New York: Garland Press).

Collins, Anthony (1990) *A Philosophical Inquiry Concerning Human Liberty* (Bristol: Thoemmes).

Davidson, Donald (1980) "Intending", in *Essays on Actions and Events* (Oxford: Clarendon Press), 83–102.

De Bary, Philip (2002) *Thomas Reid and Scepticism: His Reliabilist Response* (London: Routledge).

Duggan, Timothy (1976) "Active Power and the Liberty of Moral Agents", in *Thomas Reid: Critical Interpretations* (Philadelphia: University Science Center), 103–12.

—— (1984) "Thomas Reid on Memory, Prescience and Freedom", in V. Hope (ed.), *Philosophers of the Scottish Enlightenment* (Edinburgh: Edinburgh University Press).

Fischer, John (1994) *The Metaphysics of Free Will: An Essay on Control* (Oxford: Blackwell Press).

Fitzpatrick, William (2000) *Teleology and the Norms of Nature* (New York: Garland Press).

Frankfurt, Harry (1988) "Identification and Wholeheartedness", in *The Importance of What we Care about* (Cambridge: Cambridge University Press).

Gallie, Roger (1989) *Thomas Reid and "The Way of Ideas"* (Dordrecht: Kluwer Publishing).

Grave, Selwyn (1960) *The Scottish Philosophy of Common Sense* (Oxford: Clarendon Press).

Harris, James (2001) "Reid's Challenge to Reductionism about Human Agency" *Reid Studies*, 4/2: 33–42.

—— (2003) "On Reid's 'Inconsistent Triad': A Reply to McDermid", *British Journal for the History of Philosophy*, 11/1: 121–7.

Hazelton, Dean (1978) "On an Alleged Inconsistency in Reid's Theory of Moral Liberty", *Journal of the History of Philosophy*, 41/4: 453–5.

Hobbes, Thomas (1648) "Of Liberty and Necessity", in *The English Works of Thomas Hobbes*, iv (Aalen: Scientia).

—— (1648) "The Questions Concerning Liberty, Necessity and Chance, Clearly Stated and Debated Between Dr. Bramhall, Bishop of Derry, and Thomas Hobbes of Malmesbury", *The English Works of Thomas Hobbes*, iv (Aalen: Scientia).

—— (1994) *Leviathan* (Indianopolis: Hackett Publishing).

Hoffman, Paul, "Thomas Reid's Notion of Exertion", unpublished manuscript.

Hume, David (1995) *Enquiries Concerning Human Understanding and Concerning the Principles of Morals*, ed. L. A. Selby-Bigge and P. H. Nidditch (Oxford: Clarendon Press).

—— (2000) *Treatise of Human Nature*, ed. D. F. Norton and M. J. Norton (Oxford: Oxford University Press).

Huoranszki, Ferenc (2003) "Common Sense and the Theory of Human Behavior", in J. Haldane and S. Read (eds.), *The Philosophy of Thomas Reid* (London: Blackwell Publishing), 113–30.

Kant, Immanuel (1996) "Groundwork of the Metaphysics of Morals", in *Practical Philosophy: The Cambridge Edition of the Works of Immanuel Kant*, tr. and ed. M. J. Gregor (Cambridge: Cambridge University Press).

Lehrer, Keith (1989) *Thomas Reid* (London: Routledge).

Locke, John (1975) *An Essay Concerning Human Understanding*, ed. P. H. Nidditch (Oxford: Clarendon Press).

Lowe, E. J. (1986) "Necessity and the Will in Locke's Theory of Action", *History of Philosophy Quarterly*, 3/2: 149–63.

McDermid, Douglas (1999) "Thomas Reid on Moral Liberty and Common Sense", *British Journal for the History of Philosophy*, 7/2: 275–303.

Madden, Edward (1982) "Common Sense and Agency Theory", *Review of Metaphysics*, 36: 319–41.

Malebranche, Nicolas (1997) *The Search After Truth*, tr. and ed. T. Lennon (Cambridge: Cambridge University Press).

Molière (1968) "The Imaginary Invalid", in *The Misanthrope and Other Plays*, tr. D. M. Frame (New York: Signet Classics).

Nell, Onora (1975) *Acting on Principle: An Essay on Kantian Ethics* (New York: Columbia University Press).

Nichols, Ryan (2002) "Reid on Fictional Objects and the Way of Ideas", *Philosophical Quarterly*, 52/209: 582–601.

O'Connor, Timothy (1994) "Thomas Reid on Free Agency", *Journal for the History of Philosophy*, 32/4: 605–22.

—— (1995) "Agent Causation", in T. O'Connor (ed.), *Agents, Causes and Events: Essays on Indeterminism and Free Will* (New York: Oxford University Press), 173–200.

—— (2000) *Persons and Causes: The Metaphysics of Free Will* (New York: Oxford University Press).

Priestley, Joseph (1774) *An Examination of Dr. Reid's Inquiry into the Human Mind on the Principles of Common Sense, Dr. Beattie's Essay on the Nature and Immutability of Truth, and Dr. Oswald's Appeal to Common Sense in Behalf of Religion* (London).

—— (1976) *The Doctrine of Philosophical Necessity Illustrated* (New York: Garland Press).

Reid, Thomas (1872) *The Works of Thomas Reid, D.D.*, ed. W. Hamilton, 6th edn., 2 vols. (Edinburgh: MacLachlan & Stewart).

—— (1969) *Essays on the Active Powers of Man*, ed. B. Brody (Cambridge, Mass.: MIT Press).

—— (1990) *Practical Ethics*, ed. K. Haakonsen (Princeton: Princeton University Press).

—— (1995) *Thomas Reid on the Animate Creation: Papers Relating to the Life Sciences*, ed. P. Wood (University Park, Pa.: Pennsylvania State University Press).

—— (1997) *An Inquiry into the Human Mind: On the Principles of Common Sense*, ed. D. Brookes (University Park, Pa.: Pennsylvania State University Press).

—— (2001) "Of Power", *Philosophical Quarterly*, 51/202: 3–12.

—— (2002) *Essays on the Intellectual Powers of Man*, ed. D. Brookes (University Park, Pa.: Pennsylvania State University Press).

Rowe, William (1987) "Reid's Conception of Human Freedom", *Monist*, 70/4: 430–40.

—— (1987) "Two Concepts of Freedom", *Proceedings and Addresses of the American Philosophical Association*, Supplement 61: 43–64.

—— (1991) "Responsibility, Agent-Causation and Freedom: An Eighteenth Century View", *Ethics*, 101: 270–97.

—— (1991) *Thomas Reid on Freedom and Morality* (Ithaca, NY: Cornell University Press).

—— (2000) "The Metaphysics of Freedom: Reid's Theory of Agent Causation", *American Catholic Philosophical Quarterly*, 74/3: 425–46.

Shaftesbury, third earl of (1999) *Characteristicks of Men, Manners, Opinions, Times*, ed. Lawrence Klein (Cambridge: Cambridge University Press).

Short, T. L. (1983) "Teleology in Nature", *American Philosophical Quarterly*, 20/4: 311–20.

Smith, John C. (2000) *Companion to the Works of Philosopher Thomas Reid, 1710–1796* (Lewiston: E. Mellen Press).

Stalley, R. F. (1989) "Causality and Agency in the Philosophy of Thomas Reid", in M. Dalgarno and E. Matthews (eds.), *The Philosophy of Thomas Reid* (Dordrecht: Kluwer Academic Publishers) 275–83.

Stecker, Robert (1992) "Thomas Reid's Philosophy of Action", in *Philosophical Studies*, 66: 197–208.

Strawson, Galen (1989) *The Secret Connexion: Causation, Realism and David Hume* (Oxford: Clarendon Press).

Taylor, Richard (1966) *Action and Purpose* (Englewood Cliffs, NJ: Prentice-Hall).

Van Cleve, James (1996) "If Meinong is Wrong, is McTaggart Right?", *Philosophical Topics*, 24/1: 231–54.

Weinstock, Jerome (1975) "Reid's Definition of Freedom", *Journal of the History of Philosophy*, 13/3: 335–45.

Wolterstorff, Nicholas (2001) *Thomas Reid and the Story of Epistemology* (Cambridge: Cambridge University Press).

Woodfield, Andrew (1976) *Teleology* (Cambridge: Cambridge University Press).

Woozley, A. D. (1987) "Reid on Moral Liberty", *Monist*, 70/4: 442–52.

Wright, John (1983) *The Sceptical Realism of David Hume* (Minneapolis: University of Minnesota Press).

——(1987) "Hume vs. Reid on Ideas: The New Hume Letter", *Mind*, 96/383: 392–8.

Wright, Larry (1976) *Teleological Explanations: An Etiological Analysis of Goals and Functions* (Los Angeles: University of California Press).

Yaffe, Gideon (2000) *Liberty Worth the Name: Locke on Free Agency* (Princeton: Princeton University Press).

——(2001) "Locke on Suspending, Refraining and the Freedom to Will", *History of Philosophy Quarterly*, 18/4: 373–92.

Index

.